THE STORY TELLER

LEADERS

THE STORY TELLER

LEADERS

A Gallery of Biblical Portraits

Steve Stephens

PROMISE
PRESS

An Imprint of Barbour Publishing

Cover illustration: Lookout Design Group
                www.lookoutdesign.com

Published by Promise Press, an imprint of Barbour Publishing, Inc., P.O. Box 719, Uhrichsville, Ohio 44683, http://www.barbourbooks.com

 Member of the
Evangelical Christian
Publishers Association

Printed in the United States of America.

DEDICATION

To all who have taught me . . .
The freedom of Bondage-Breaker,
The generosity of Land-Giver,
The patience of People-Builder.

ACKNOWLEDGMENTS

The author gratefully acknowledges those whose lives and support have been integral to retelling the stories of Bondage-Breaker and Land-Giver and People-Builder.

- Tami, for being a supportive wife and listening and reading all the rough drafts. You are the lady of my dreams.

- Mom and Dad, for always being there.

- Sue Powers and Linda Graham, for patiently typing and retyping.

- The New Vision Class and all those who listened to these stories as they took shape.

- The Thursday Night Dinner Group (Gary and Debra, Roy and Joyce, Greg and Karen), for sharing their lives.

- David Sanford, for believing in this project and constantly encouraging me.

- Paul Ingram, for his brilliant creativity and expert editing.

- Alice Gray, for being so kind and positive.

- John VanDiest, for his confidence in me as an author.

- Susan Schlabach and all the wonderful people at Promise Press.

- My old friends, Jerry and Rick, wherever you might be.

INTRODUCTION

The Bible is the ultimate book.

It is a panorama of hope and freedom, love and heroism, discovery and adventure and victory. Most important, it is about walking with the one beyond the sky who holds the stars in his hands.

Leaders retells the events of the exodus from the Land of Pyramids and the wanderings through a wilderness toward a bountiful land. But entering that land meant facing what seemed to be impossible odds. And once the land was entered and won, life continued to be a struggle, as people forgot People-Builder. Thirty stories cover centuries—generations of fascinating men and women:

General and Point Man.

Innkeeper and Beekeeper's Wife.

Lion and Left Hand and Loner.

These lives touch the heart, because these were real people like us, who were appointed to walk through a strange and sometimes frightening time. Some say the Old Testament lacks relevance in a computer age, but the more you know of these people, the more the Old Testament becomes today.

So I approach this book with a storyteller's heart, but a scholar's respect. I want to make the events vivid, while remaining faithful to fact and chronology.

Leaders continues the story begun in *Beginnings*. It can be read in sequence or alone. If you enjoy these stories, look for *Kingdoms*, and *Promises*.

As you step into these stories, remember what General said as he stood at the mountain so long ago:

> *Bury these words in your heart and mind.*
> *Keep them close to your hands and head.*
> *Teach them to your children—*
> *when you are at home or on the road,*
> *when you go to bed and when you get up.*

PART 1
BONDAGE-BREAKER

TABLE OF CONTENTS
BONDAGE-BREAKER

PROLOGUE

The circle was tight to ward off the evening's chill breeze. A crystal moon stared, full and unblinking, on they who sat cross-legged by the fire in the great desert of the blue planet. The old man with the long, grey beard and a hundred wrinkles stood tall and straight and proud, so close he almost seemed part of the yellow tongues of flame at the circle center. His shadow flickered and danced across the skins of the near-by tents.

The old man reached into the shadows for the small-necked goat's skin, filled with clear water. Old hands lifted the skin in mid-air above his parched lips, as a stream descended into his open mouth.

But now the people gasped in horror; for he turned the skin away and quietly watched the stream of precious water cascade onto the dry, sandy ground. The earth swallowed its gift. The old man pulled a hand-carved oaken walking stick from beneath his plain wool robe and stirred the wet sand into a small patch of mud. He bent down, gathered a lump of moist dirt and carefully rolled it into a ball.

Ancient hands shaped the soil.

His movements held meaning only the older ones understood.

The children, who would be punished for wasting water, watched earnestly. This night's lesson must be important indeed.

From his bag he slipped a small handful of rye stalks, well dried into straw. Wordlessly, meticulously, unhurriedly his wrinkled fingers kneaded straw into mud and shaped the mixture into a small block. Facing the flames, he balanced the block on a flat piece of wood and set his fashioned brick into the embers.

"Ten thousand bricks.

"Ten million bricks.

"Mixed, formed in molds, dried in the furnace sun. Millions of bricks to stoop each back, to the song of the whip. Lives poured out into the sand in an alien land."

They leaned forward to watch and listen and remember their history as water hissed from the brick. In a little while it began to harden.

The old man threw a handful of powder into the flames. WHOOOSH. Adults jumped and children screamed. Fire exploded into a mountain of smoke and sparks. The cloud faded, but a triangle of smoke lingered. It almost looked like a monument of the ancient Land of Pyramids.

"Brick upon brick; stone upon stone. Row upon never-ending row. Cities rise and pyramid tombs swallow generations of kings," said the ancient storyteller. "And a people in bondage are bowed lower and lower into the dust."

The image faded and the few rubbed their eyes. "Do you wish me to tell you how the bondage was broken?" asked the man. The people nodded their heads enthusiastically.

"You will have to learn new names for the one who lives beyond the sky and holds the stars in his hands. You know him as Garden-Maker and as Promise-Keeper. Now you must see him as Bondage-Breaker, for thus he has shown himself to our people."

The old man turned toward the fire and reached into the flames with metal tongs to grab hold of the red-heated brick. He held the glowing block above his head and proclaimed, "The story begins with this!"

Then he threw the brick into the air and watched it shatter as it hit the packed ground outside the circle. A thousand glowing sparks shared the expanse with far-away stars. It looked almost as if the heavens themselves were falling.

"Hope is reborn when Bondage-Breaker reaches down," he began.

A MOTHER'S LOVE
SECURES A CHILD'S FUTURE
EVEN IF IT MEANS
LETTING GO.

CHAPTER 1

THE BABY

T hey're dangerous."

"They're slaves," scoffed Delta King as he looked down into a deep valley quarry where olive-skinned men strained against massive blocks of stone. Sweating backs glistened in the midday furnace.

"They look like slaves," said the ancient serpent. "They are more."

The snake who spoke was Shining One,
who had outshone the stars,
who had glowed with elegant majesty,
whose radiance had been the most beautiful of any angel.

Now the glow was mostly shadow, though he did cast a hint of shimmer about him. The gleam sparked in eyes deep and dark and dangerous. Only the gleam remained, but in the darkness of Delta King's mind it looked ablaze with promise.

The gleam now was scornfully cast toward his companion.

"They're dangerous, because they walk with Promise-Keeper."

"So what?"

"These slaves of the eastern delta are of Merchant and Wrestler. Promise-Keeper has planted freedom in their hearts. They were twelve sons just few centuries ago. Now look. Soon you will cut stone in their pits."

The Delta King looked to the fertile flatlands in the distance. Uncountable sun-baked brick hovels dotted the plain. His friend made a troubling point.

"The census counted more than a million of them."

"They will multiply," whispered the snake, "until they become stronger than the people of the Delta."

"What should I do?"

"Whatever you like. You are the powerful Delta King, aren't you? Don't you hold their feeble lives in your grasp? Just close your fingers . . . and squeeze."

The snake could see that no more persuasion was needed. He pressed his program home.

"Work them like animals.

"Beat their backs bloody when they don't keep pace.

"Bleed their souls dry of hope and heart and heritage."

The snake was right, thought Delta King. These slaves would learn. No promises would be kept for them. Their deaths would become his victory. He doubled the work of the descendants of Wrestler. They dug deep canals connecting the channels of the Wide River. They built thick walls for new cities and silos for grain to feed them.

The strong moved great blocks of stone. The weak and young filled molds with clay and straw and set the shaped blocks in the sun to bake. Millions of bricks to stack into temples and tombs and monuments.

Here was immortality—more and more magnificent buildings than any other king had raised. In the process the slaves would weary and break and die.

Weary indeed were the descendants of Wrestler. Long hours under blistering sun were sustained by little-enough food and less water and sleep. The people of the Delta seemed more and more cruel with demands past toleration. Life was bitter and unfair.

But the slaves did not break.

They became harder of mettle and stronger of body.

They grew more numerous.

"The spirit of Wrestler is mighty," said Delta King.

"Your spirit is soft," hissed the snake. "Humans are frail little flowers. There are many ways to pluck them from the soil. You must simply tug at their roots; deal with their babies."

"How?"

"Kill the boys. Let the girls grow up beautiful and vain. Lure them from the old ways so they can find husbands among the Delta people. Soon. . . ," the snake slowly coiled into a relaxed heap to sun, "no more children of Wrestler."

"Oh, and don't forget," he added with a yawn and grin that unsheathed razor sharp fangs. "Take the most beautiful for yourself."

Delta King hastened to assemble the slave midwives at the palace.

"When a boy child is born, see that he doesn't let out his first cry," the King warned. "Cut his cord and take his breath and rush him away to burn with the stubble. If you hear a newborn noise among the slave houses, call for the soldiers. They will silence the sounds of boy children."

"We cannot do such a thing!" gasped the midwives.

"It is murder."

"It is an abomination to Promise-Keeper."

"Think of it as survival," said the king. "Disobey even once, and your bodies will be burned with the rest."

Downcast midwives walked deliberately from the palace. Their lowered faces hid fear and anger and fierce resolve.

"Do as you wish," said one. "But no baby will die at my hand."

"We must stand as one. We must not kill babies."

They returned to their villages and looked to Promise-Keeper for protection. The hot desert wind whistled from the west and into their midst. In its breath rode reassuring phrases. Those who listened were sure it was the voice of Promise-Keeper himself.

"Yours are life-bringing arms," sang the wind, "hands that bring forth the future. Fear not, for I am with you. Bring life so that your sons grow up valiant and vigorous. Among them I will give you a prince."

Remarkably hardy infants were born that year. Fewer fell to disease, and none died to satisfy the king's blood thirst.

Inevitably soldiers arrived at the midwives' doors. They were herded, not so courteously as before, into the palace chamber.

"Have you disobeyed me?" the king raged.

"The daughters of Wrestler are unlike other women. They do not need midwives. They birth in secret, before we hear of their pains."

"So take the babies from them."

"And how are we weak women to wrestle an infant from the work-hardened arms of a mother, and past her husband and brothers? They would kill us before we could get close."

"I should wash this floor with your disobedient blood," Delta King screamed. Now the women expected that guards would slash them down. But no one moved except the red-faced king in his harangue. He finally collapsed into his throne, exhausted.

"Get out of my sight, and may you die a miserable death."

The midwives were thrown from the palace chamber. The great doors closed hard behind them. They were relieved, yet they knew the worst was to come. But on the wind they had heard the voice of Promise-Keeper. Now they had seen his protecting hand. Never would they doubt his power and presence.

The next day messengers roamed the slave villages of the eastern delta. The command of Delta King thundered through the Land of Pyramids.

Every slave boy child must die. Each male baby descended from Wrestler must be killed. Thus we will purge this inferior race that refuses to honor and worship the sun and land and river that sustain life. Families harboring infant boys will be destroyed without mercy. All who fail to report an infant cry will be drowned in the arms of the Wide River. Absolute obedience is required of all.

The words had been expected. Still, all the slaves mourned. All knew of the plot of the king and the stand of the midwives. All had debated how to protect the children.

The soldiers' harsh knock was heard now, sometimes followed by the wails of parents. But for all the king's efforts to hunt down the helpless infants, many a secret place in home and field and cave silently sheltered tiny enemies of the land.

In one such flatland house, a boy and a girl already were nurtured on the stories of the Man and Woman in the garden, Builder and the rainbow, Merchant and the new land. Father and grandfather spoke of how Dreamer rose to greatness in the Delta. Each detail was committed to memory.

The stories provided perspective and hope when the painful present seemed heavy. When the father heard the executive command of Delta King, he threw down his tools and ran home to embrace his wife. The two held each other and wept for the new life that was rounding her belly.

"How could something so evil be happening?" cried the father.

"This is the work of Shining One," said the mother. "His ways are built upon lies and strewn with death. He fears us. I do not understand why."

20

"Joyfully he will wield Delta King's sword to sever the line of Wrestler."

"Then there is no hope?"

The father smiled. "With Promise-Keeper there is always hope and there is ultimately victory. If our child is a son, we will ask Promise-Keeper to guard and strengthen and plant freedom deep in his heart."

"That is much to ask even of Promise-Keeper," his wife mused.

"Much to ask the one who holds the stars in his hands? I will ask though the world be filled with delta kings."

"It is a boy, beautiful and healthy," whispered the midwife under the darkness of night in a secluded place near the village. Here a new baby could wail away without fear. This son was unusually handsome and hearty and full of promise. In his tiny, dark nursery hideaway at home, the parents muffled his cries and held him extra close. Brother and sister kept watch for soldiers and untrustworthy neighbors. Any hint of this male child's existence could mean death for all of them. For a hundred days the mother nursed her infant in fear, but as he grew strong and raucous, it was more difficult to keep him secret.

Early one morning while darkness kept its final hold over land and water, the seven-year-old daughter slipped from the small brick house and made her way to the marshlands along the banks of the Wide River. Wading barefoot into the shallow water she disappeared into a graceful forest of reeds where the mature plants were twice as tall as the tallest man and seemed as thick as her father's arm. With a large knife she cut as many young stalks as she could carry. She and her mother would weave these reeds into a sturdy basket.

The next day before the beginning of the dawn, mother and daughter stole away from the small brick house and made their way to the marshlands along the banks of the Wide River. Now they carried their new basket, which had been blackened with pitch. Carefully they set the basket afloat in a secluded thicket of reeds and tied it to the largest stalk in case it floated free. Kissing her baby brother on his cheek the girl whispered, "I love you," and kept watch from a rock-strewn gully a short distance from the shore.

The girl dozed as the sun rose above the eastern mountains of the desert wilderness. She was startled to wakefulness as the day grew hot. People were coming along the river toward her brother's hiding place. At the center of this giggling knot of girls walked a lithe, regal-looking young woman. The unexpected parade came closer, closer, ever closer. It was too late to retrieve the basket without being seen. "Oh please keep him from crying," she begged Promise-Keeper. "Please help them not to notice."

But the group paused not a dozen paces from the basket's hiding place. The one at the center held herself like a beautiful princess. She gracefully removed her fine robes and stepped into the cool water. As she washed, a small muffled whimper drifted down river. She silently surveyed the reeds. One had to be careful of snakes and other dangerous river creatures.

"What is that?" she asked her servants. "There in the marsh."

Servant girls came running up with the floating basket. "It's a tiny boat," said one of the servants. "Look at its cargo," giggled another, pulling back the blanket covering.

"A baby!" the princess gasped as she tried to comfort the child.

"He has been abandoned by the descendants of Wrestler."

"I wonder," said the princess, glancing over the rocks and hills. She gently lifted him from his basket and rocked him in her arms and hummed a lullaby.

His cry stopped.

His eyes opened.

His tiny hand reached for her.

She smiled and ran her fingers across his tiny face. The infant seemed to smile in return.

"What an amazing child," the princess sighed. She leaned down and kissed his forehead.

"It is a boy," a servant girl said with anxiety. "We must take him to the soldiers."

"And watch them split him open?" asked the princess. "The river has given us this special child. I will allow no one to harm him."

An older servant looked doubtful. "The infant is charming, but Delta King said there will be no exceptions."

"I will speak to my father," said the princess. "I insist this exception to his awful law."

"The baby seems hungry," said a shy girl who seemed to have appeared out of nowhere among the women. "Would you like me to find a slave woman to nurse him?"

The princess regarded her. "That would be good," she said.

Her mother looked up in horror as the sister burst into the hut. "Our baby is found by Delta King's daughter. She says she will protect him."

The girl babbled on excitedly until the strained woman broke into tears, comprehending the news. "Promise-Keeper has protected my son," she whispered.

" . . . And the princess asked me to find a nursing woman."

At the river the daughter silently presented her mother to the princess.

"I have brought the best slave nurse in the Delta," said the daughter.

"I thought you might," said the princess with a laugh. "I need you to care for this baby who is to be my son. I will give you an order to show to anyone who comes demanding the child. Send word if there is a problem with the soldiers. I will pay you well, but keep him secret until I come for him."

"I will care for him as if he were my own son," answered the mother.

SPEAK AND ACT AS IF EVERY WORD AND DEED WILL SOMEDAY BE PUBLIC. LIKELY THEY WILL.

CHAPTER 2

THE KILLING

Y ou have hidden a slave child?" stammered the delta-king. "Where?"

"This baby is special. I will not tell you."

"He must die; that is my command. He is a descendant of Wrestler, a threat to us all."

"Not if he is one of us. He would be the son you have not borne."

This argument ultimately won. The baby and his nurse moved to the royal palace. Here he learned to walk and talk and act like the People of the Pyramids. Tutors taught him to swim the Wide River and ride horses and shoot a bow. The most gifted men of the land came to the palace to educate the king's son in the wisdom of the time.

He began with reading and writing and the calculation of numbers.

He moved on to philosophy and the history of the ancient delta-kings.

He mastered intricacies of administering people and laws and strategies of war.

The king's son excelled in these studies and remained the favorite of Delta King, even after another male child was born to one of his wives.

But what interested the child most were stories he learned from his slave mother. He learned the promise of the rainbow: *No matter how distant Promise-Keeper seems, he is always close and he always cares.*

He also learned the promise of his people: *Promise-Keeper will give the descendants of Merchant a new land that would stretch as far as eyes could see in all directions.*

The king's son hid these promises deep in his heart and never forgot them.

As a young man he rose in the ranks to command Delta King's army and earned the name of General. When the land to the south invaded the

Land of Pyramids, the king's son won the decisive battle and rid his country of its enemy. But even as he enjoyed a hero's welcome, the king's son felt discontent. His own people remained in bitter slavery.

"It's not right," he said one evening as he visited with his brother in the slave village. "I sit in a palace of luxury. You do hard labor from dawn to dark, with scarcely food to survive."

"Promise-Keeper is with us," said the brother. "Someday we'll be free to return to the Valley of Apples and the new land."

"Delta King will never let you leave."

"When the time is right he won't be able to stop us."

As the king's son thought about these things his admiration for the slaves grew. So did his resentment for the people of the delta. As the seasons passed, the king's son reached out to Promise-Keeper.

One morning, before the servants woke, he heard the soft words: "Come walk."

Looking into the darkness he asked, "Where will you take me?"

"Beyond the palace walls and away from the river," came the whisper.

So as the sun lingered on the horizon, General walked and talked and poured out his heart.

"What would you like?" asked Promise-Keeper.

"I'd like my people to be free."

"That is also my desire."

"Then why don't you do something about it?"

"I will."

"When?" demanded the king's son.

"When you have learned all you must learn," whispered the wind. "Be patient and your wishes will become reality."

The king's son started to ask one more question, but the wind was calm and the morning silent.

The king's son now walked each dawn with Promise-Keeper, but his impatience and anger grew.

During the son's fortieth summer he visited his slave brother again in the northern Delta. His brother had become a respected and eloquent leader among the descendants of Wrestler. He had a kind-hearted wife and four sons who loved their royal relative. Together they spoke of injustice and freedom. At the right time Promise-Keeper would lead his people to the new land.

For two days they spoke and dreamed and drew close. On the morning of the third day the king's son left his brother's family. But he did not return home. Instead he walked the quarries and building sites. He saw pain in the faces of slaves and he saw cruelty in the faces of the slave drivers. His own face was a mask of anguish.

As the golden disc climbed to the roof of the blue sky and pounded down on the bare backs of the slave men, the guards drove the slaves harder. When a man hesitated, he was beaten. If he complained, he was killed.

The king's son clenched his fist as his anger built and he cried out to the sky, "Why do you allow this? Are you blind or heartless? Or is this beyond your power?"

"My heart is broken," whispered the wind, "and when the time is right my people will be free."

"But what about now!" the king's son yelled.

He heard a gruff demanding voice behind a nearby hill, "Faster! Run, I say, run faster!"

The king's son crested the hill and saw a large muscular guard beating a young slave boy whose arms were loaded with bricks. The boy was bent over and the guard struck him again and again with a thick wooden club. The slave swirled and stumbled as the blows rained onto his head and shoulders and back.

"STOP!" demanded the king's son. "Leave the boy alone."

The guard looked up and called, "Whoever you are, be on your way. This worthless animal will soon learn to obey." He resumed the beating.

The boy staggered on as the blows increased in ferocity. Blood covered the slave's back. The boy fell to the ground and the guard aimed a kick to the stomach.

But it missed the mark when a muscular arm propelled the man backward, lifting him almost off his feet. "You are speaking to the son of Delta King and general of the army."

"I'm simply doing my job," sputtered the guard, his eyes on the blade poised inches from his throat.

"Can't you see that you are killing him? You have hit him enough."

"He must work or he must die. Put away your sword, son of the king. Go back to the palace and leave this to me."

The guard turned toward the boy, who had not moved. "Get up!" he yelled and kicked the slave once more in the stomach.

The king's son's face went red and his sword hand trembled. He looked in all directions. They were alone. Then he gripped his sword with both hands and expertly swung the flat of its blade into the guard's side with rib-cracking force. The taskmaster yelled in pain, turned and charged—into the waiting thrust. His own lunge propelled the blade through heart and lungs. He shuddered and went limp, falling beside the boy, who looked in amazement into the blank, lifeless stare. The king's son jerked his sword free and cleaned the blade of blood on the dead guard's tunic.

The boy climbed to his feet, looked at the body and then at the king's son.

"Don't say anything about this," demanded the king's son.

The boy shook his head fearfully and ran away.

Nearby Shining One hissed with satisfaction and slowly slithered beneath the slave driver's body. *If Promise-Keeper had plans for this prince, they have come to nothing,* he thought gleefully.

The king's son dug a shallow grave in the hot sand with his sword. He quickly rolled the body in and covered it. No one had come into sight. He turned back toward his brother's house, still clenching his teeth behind bloodless lips.

The next morning as the king's son was leaving the community, he saw a slave hitting another slave. "You have enough enemies," he yelled. "Why hurt each other?"

The larger man turned with a sneer. "What right do you have to correct us? If we don't listen, will you bury our bodies next to the overseer?"

The king's son's face turned white and he walked away quickly. His heart pounded fast. How did they know? The boy had told and word had spread. Soon it would reach ears of Delta King's spies.

As the search for the missing overseer commenced, little torture was needed to learn the truth. When Delta King heard what had happened, he disowned his son and sentenced him to death. No slave-born, even one in high places, could kill one of the people of the delta. Order was at stake.

But the execution couldn't proceed, because the king's son was missing. He fled east into the desolate lands beyond the bitter lakes. For a week General walked into the wilderness, and on the afternoon of the seventh day he stopped at a small oasis with a well and several palm trees.

As he rested, exhausted in the shade, seven sisters came to the well with their sheep. "May I bring you some water?" asked one of the young women.

"Thank you," said General.

A moment later she returned with a drink and then she helped her sisters draw water for the flock.

General watched the woman who'd brought him a drink. Her eyes sparkled and her smile was kind. She joked with her sisters in carefree intimacy.

Suddenly a herd of camels burst into the oasis and scattered the women's sheep. General grabbed a camel herder who was pushing the women from the water. "What are you doing?" he demanded as he gripped the man's shoulders.

"Watering our animals," said the man.

"Someone is using the well. I think you might wait your turn." General stared into the man's eyes and fingered the sword strapped to his side. "When they finish, you will have plenty."

The man noticed the sword and agreed. The men retreated and General helped the sisters gather and finish watering their sheep.

The woman with sparkling eyes came to General. "You are a man of courage. Where is your home?"

"I am a wanderer."

"Every person needs a home," said the woman with a smile.

The sisters returned home and the woman with the sparkling eyes told her father the happenings at the well.

"Where is this man?"

"At the oasis."

"Go and get him," ordered the father. "I wish to meet a man of courage and fairness. Such is rare in this land."

That night General enjoyed a meal of lamb that kindled a friendship. He also felt the first stirrings of admiration that would soon grow to love. In time he married the woman with the sparkling eyes and raised two sturdy sons.

Forty summers he walked with Promise-Keeper each morning.

Forty summers he tended the flocks of his father-in-law.

Forty summers he remembered the pain of his people.

One morning as General walked with Promise Keeper he heard a mournful cry.

"What has happened?" asked General as he stopped in place.

"Their pain is great and now they have turned to me," came the reply.

"Is it time?"

"It is time," said a voice that made General tremble.

FACED WITH DIFFICULTY
BEYOND ABILITY,
FEAR MUST SUBMIT
TO FAITH

CHAPTER 3

THE CALL

It is time!"

The words of Promise-Keeper echoed in the mind of General as he tended his sheep. He had led the flock a day north to a place of pasture in the sparse wilderness land. Here were hidden streams. The grass was tender, the sheep contented.

He ate his evening meal under the stars. The immense craggy mountain glowed in bright moonlight. Enormous, troubling thoughts of his birthland filled his mind as he huddled near a meager fire of juniper wood.

The sheep were quiet.

Earth and sky coalesced.

The desert stillness was almost a living thing.

Yet now he felt neither alone nor lonely. It was almost as if he shared his firelight with an unseen wanderer.

What looked like lightning flashed from a cloudless sky illuminating the mountain for an instant. Flames erupted higher up the slope on which he camped. It looked to be a short walk away, though the clear mountain air distorted the look of distance. It was an odd sight to behold. There'd been no storm. No other fire builders had been seen. And this fire seemed neither to die down nor become brighter as if it was being fed. Perhaps it was bandits who watched him and would try to take his sheep. But no, they would not set a fire he could see. This looked like a signal fire.

And now it signalled to him.

Only fools walked those treacherous rocks in the dark. He knew that. But General felt strangely drawn to leave his safe firelight and climb.

Well over a mile he walked uphill and around boulders. He stumbled onto a sort of path that led toward his destination. The full moon was sufficient to light his night journey. And the fire he wanted to see was definitely closer now.

At last he reached a small plateau, barren but for a large, misplaced thorn bush. This bush was indeed unusual. It was engulfed by intense, steady flame that neither grew brighter nor dimmed. Flames danced among the leaves and limbs, but somehow the bush did not shrivel into ash. Its wood did not char.

This is impossible, thought General as he moved closer.

"Stop!" boomed a familiar voice.

He swung about in a full circle, almost tripping over the folds of his cloak in his astonished fright. But no one stepped from the shadows. In less than a moment he had peered beyond the bush, but no one was on the other side.

"Remove your sandals," ordered the voice. "The earth around this fire is set apart. This is a most special place for I am here."

The intensity of the voice drove General to his knees. He stared at the bush for another moment then quietly and obediently pulled his sandal straps over his heels. He never took his eyes from the fire until he was barefoot. Then he lay face down with arms stretched toward the bush in the position of intense worship.

"I hold the stars in my hand.

"I am Garden-Maker.

"I am Promise-Keeper."

General moved back to his knees and covered his eyes. "I cannot look into the face of the one who lives beyond the sky. Have mercy or I will die."

"I have heard the cries of my people. It is time to free them from their oppressors," said the voice. "Long ago I promised a new land to Merchant, a good and spacious land, a land of blessing and peace."

"I know the old stories of the City of Palms and the Place of the Portal and the Valley of Apples."

General uncovered his eyes but kept his face bent toward his feet. He felt the heat of the fire as it bathed his body.

"So now you will bring my people out of the land where they are oppressed. You are to take them into this land that is already theirs."

Now he looked up in astonishment, despite himself.

"I can't do that," said General. "I'm a shepherd, an *old* shepherd. Perhaps forty summers ago I could have done something. Not now."

"You can do more than you know, if I am beside you. Trust me, and the People of the Promise will stand by this mountain within a year."

"I don't know what to say to them," argued General.

"Tell them Garden-Maker and Promise-Keeper has sent you to free them from the power of Delta King. Tell them I send you to take them to the new land. If they ask for more, tell them I will give them another name to call me. They shall call me Bondage-Breaker, for I am able to break their bonds and show them true freedom."

"What if they won't listen to me? How can I get their attention?"

"What's in your hand?" asked the fire.

"My shepherd's staff."

"Throw it to the ground."

General obeyed and when the staff hit the earth it turned into a serpent. He jumped back as the venomous snake hissed and showed its fangs.

"Don't be afraid," said Bondage-Breaker. "Reach out and grab its tail."

As General touched the tail, the snake once again became a staff.

"This is a sign to show my people and Delta King that you are their leader, and that I am beside you. Now place your hand inside your cloak."

General did as he was told.

"Now take it out," said the fire.

All the color had drained out of his hand until it was sick and wasted and white. Large blisters and open sores covered palm and fingers. General gasped.

"Place your hand back in your cloak and take it out."

When he did this his hand was tan and normal. He held his two hands side by side, and saw that there was no difference.

"If they still doubt, take a cup of water from the Wide River. Pour it onto the sand. The water in the cup will be clear, but it will become blood as it soaks into the ground, as my people's blood has soaked into the delta sand."

"These signs will get their attention," said General, "but I won't be able to keep it. I'm not good with words. My tongue grows thick when I speak before many."

"I will whisper in your ear the words you need. I will calm your spirit, so that your words will be smooth. I will give you power to speak so that it will be the same as if I spoke."

Forty summers of hiding in fear. The shepherd stood and faced the fire in frustration.

"It isn't what you can do that I question. I can't do this. There are others who can."

The flame turned to a pure white. General staggered back and covered his eyes.

"I could choose another, but I choose you. I also have summoned your brother. He left the Land of Pyramids this day and walks across the desert. He will stand with you before Delta King to say what you cannot."

There was a moment of silence. The voice spoke again: "I do not bargain. Servant or rebel; which are you?"

There was a coldness to the words. They gave gooseflesh as if he suddenly had been thrown into a pool of water on this chilled night.

The next words were the hardest General would ever say, for he had an idea of what they meant.

"I will do whatever you ask."

"And I will be beside you," said the voice in the flame.

The earth cloaked itself in blackness. Suddenly the fire was simply gone. General stood, barefoot and alone. He could see the thorn bush in the moonlight. It was green and healthy.

General drove his sheep south toward the oasis. His father-in-law was a wise man who listened quietly. He placed his hands solemnly on the head of General and gave his blessing. In another day General and his wife and their grown sons set out toward the Land of Pyramids. General sacrificed a spotless, newborn lamb to Bondage-Breaker as a token of gratitude.

Beyond the sky, he who is infinite and eternal and all-powerful smiled.

The next day they saw a lone figure moving toward them through the heat. General stopped and squinted, then ran to greet his brother with a firm embrace.

"It's been a long time," said his brother as he kissed his cheek. "A lot has changed. The old Delta King, your adopted father, is dead. There's a new Delta King."

"And our parents?"

The Brother hesitated. "Dead many years ago."

"Our sister?"

"She is a fine mother to our people. She teaches the stories of Garden-Maker and Promise-Keeper. But the new Delta King is even more cruel and life is worse. But I imagine that the killing is forgotten."

"I imagine I am forgotten."

"No," said the Brother. "You are a hero in stories told to our children. For years our people have waited for the return of General, our avenger and the one who would set them free."

"I am not hero nor avenger nor revolutionary. I am an old shepherd."

The two men talked late into the night. General shared all Promise-Keeper had told him from the flaming thorn bush. Early the next morning they arose and walked together beside Bondage-Breaker. A week later the two brothers stood in an open field before their sister and the wisest, most respected of Wrestler's descendants. General's brother spoke with eloquence and answered their questions. He threw down his brother's staff and displayed the ashen hand and poured blood upon the sand. When the people saw these signs they accepted Promise-Keeper's new name and told the brothers they would quietly begin preparing the people for their journey.

They knew that, within the space of a day, spies would tell Delta King what had been said in the assembly. So early the next morning the brothers walked with Bondage-Breaker to the City of the Sun, passed through the majestic granite gates and took the path toward Delta King's palace.

A HARD HEART
BRINGS DISASTER,
BUT BLAMES EACH LOSS
ON EVERYTHING
BUT STUBBORNNESS.

CHAPTER 4

THE DISASTERS

Let the people go!"

The brothers, tall and weathered and hardened by labor, said the words in the audience hall of Delta King's palace.

"Who dares make such a command?" The question echoed off the red granite walls and massive limestone columns.

"Bondage-Breaker," said the one in the garb of a desert dweller. "Bondage-Breaker made the Wide River; he made the land; he made the sky. He made delta kings."

"I will not let the slaves go," said Delta King. "Rather, I will punish them for listening to fantasies of freedom."

That day the work of the slaves increased. Beatings became more brutal. The people begged General and his brother to stay away from Delta King. "Your help is killing us."

General walked with Bondage-Breaker. "What shall I do?"

"Obey," came the wind.

"But I have made matters worse. They no longer want freedom."

"They want freedom. They fear the cost."

Once again the brothers stood in the audience hall of Delta King.

"Let the people go!"

"I would rather watch you die."

"You can kill us, but the name of Bondage-Breaker is not so easy to destroy."

"Why should I care about Bondage-Breaker?"

"He rules the river, the land, the sky."

"Prove it!" scoffed the king.

The brother threw the shepherd's staff to the floor. A serpent writhed and hissed.

Delta King snapped his fingers. Sorcerers of Shining One stepped into the room and threw down staffs. These also turned into vipers. The vipers circled General's serpent, preparing to strike. Their quarry coiled and waited while the two positioned themselves on either side. They struck as one lightning bolt, but General's snake was not there, so they sank their fangs into one another. General's serpent leisurely circled the dazed attackers and swallowed them whole. Brother picked up the serpent and it became a staff again, no different than before.

"Get out," shouted the red-faced Delta King. "Do you fools think magic tricks will sway me?"

The next morning the brothers met Delta King as he walked along the Wide River. "Let the people go!" they repeated.

"You have more snakes?" he asked with a nervous laugh.

"Bondage-Breaker will touch the river and it will thicken like blood."

Brother took the shepherd's staff and touched the river. That day the water flooded its banks and doubled and tripled in size. The water thickened and turned scarlet. The red flood polluted streams and canals. Crimson mud lay deep on fields. Houses built close to the bank were swept away.

The waters had been filled with a red algae that spread with impossible speed, choking the fish and turning the land putrid. Dead fish covered the ground where the flood receded, rotting in the hot afternoon sun. No one could drink from the foul water or bathe in it.

For seven days the stench grew. Then the brothers approached Delta King. "Let the people go!"

"The river is your doing?" sneered the king. "I do not believe you have such power."

Brother waved the staff toward the soggy red plains. Pools left by the flood teemed with tiny tadpoles who grew strong on the nurturing algae. Overnight their legs popped out and tails dropped off and a bag of skin developed below each mouth. Within a cycle of the sun their raspy croaks split the night. The contaminated water now drove the frogs from the river. In great waves they hopped into the city. In the palace the sound deafened.

Frogs in beds.

Frogs on tables.

Frogs in grain bins.

Frogs squished beneath sandals. Dead frogs that began to stink. There was no escape. The people called for relief to the river gods, without relief.

The king called for the brothers.

"Enough. Remove the frogs from my city. I will let your people go."

"Bondage-Breaker is witness to your promise," said General. "Tomorrow he will lift his finger from the river and the frogs will die."

The next day people gathered and threw piles of dead frogs into the streets, piles higher than a person's height. The stench smothered the city until slaves with carts cleared the roads. When the frogs were gone, a messenger appeared before the brothers:

"I have reconsidered the agreement you tricked me into making.

"Our gods have saved us from this strange disaster.

"Your people will not leave the Land of the Delta."

Brother took the staff and struck the bank of the Wide River. Tiny eggs hatched in the stagnant pools left by the flood. Hordes of mosquitoes swarmed across the land in black clouds.

Animals went mad. People covered every part of their bodies with mud or clothing, but the mosquitoes found exposed skin. The old and sick began dying with incurable infections and in every house someone burned with fever.

Soon the mosquitoes died. The people were relieved, but the story spread of two slaves who cursed the land. Who was this Bondage-Breaker, who cared for slaves? What would he touch next?

The brothers again confronted the delta-king.

"Let the people go!"

"Never!" said the king.

"How many more disasters must there be before you let my people go?"

"I will never let your people go."

"Bondage-Breaker has touched the waters," General said. "Next he will touch the land. You will know this is his work if only the people of the Delta are judged. Wrestler's descendants will be spared."

Bondage-Breaker touched the land.

Maggots that infested the dying frogs became flies.

The flies grew fat and swarmed into the houses and even the palace.

These flies were ferocious, and their bite was painful. No one could sleep; no one could work. Flies buzzed into eyes and noses and mouths. Life became miserable for the People of the Pyramids. But it was true—Wrestler's descendants seemed unaffected.

The king called for the brothers.

"Remove the flies," he said as slaves beat the air to relieve him. "Your people can go."

"Bondage-Breaker has heard your promise," said General. "He will lift his finger."

The next day the flies disappeared. Delta King immediately forgot that they had existed.

"Let the people go!" demanded the brothers.

"No!" said the delta-king.

"Then Bondage-Breaker will return his finger to the land."

"The flies are gone. I won't change my mind."

The next day another generation of flies feasted on the rotting carcasses of the frogs. Now they carried the deadly anthrax disease to the cattle in the fields outside the city. The cattle became shaky. Their breathing grew heavy. They fell to the ground and were too weak to get to their feet. The People of the Pyramids tried to help their animals, but one by one the cattle stopped breathing. Delta King tightened his jaw. "I don't care what Bondage-Breaker does, I will never let those people go!"

Within a few days flies returned to the city. There were not nearly so many, but now the fly bites left ugly red welts that became infected and inflamed. Open sores turned into black, burning abscesses. Delta King continued his stubborn denial.

A month of this misery passed. Again the brothers met Delta King on the banks of the Wide River.

"Let the people go!"

"Never!"

"Bondage-Breaker rules the water and has touched it with three disasters.

"Bondage-Breaker rules the land and has touched it with three disasters.

"Now he will touch the sky. At this time tomorrow the Land of Pyramids will experience the power of Bondage-Breaker."

The next day jagged bolts ripped from angry clouds with explosions of thunder. Those outside ran for cover. Hailstones the size of a man's fist crashed to the ground, bouncing off the streets and pocking mud brick and roof plaster. Suddenly the sky came alive with shattering spheres of ice.

Those outside were beaten to death as they ran. Weak walls crumbled under the battering. Inside strong buildings people trembled in terror beneath what protection they could find.

Animals in the fields were killed.

Trees were shattered and crops cut to pieces.

Outdoor ovens for cooking food stood cracked and ruined.

The ground was layered in ice and debris, but still the storm continued. Now even stronger walls cracked, and roofs gave way. When the clouds moved away, bypassing the villages of the slaves, the City of the Sun and much of the land lay ruined.

During it all Delta King had paced his palace nervously. His great stone building quivered and sections of roof fell. "Bring General and his brother," he shouted over the din.

The brothers already waited at the entrance to the audience hall.

"Let the people go!" they said simply.

"I will," said Delta King, "if only Bondage-Breaker closes up the sky."

Bondage-Breaker removed his finger from the sky. Thunder and lightning stilled. Hail stopped falling. Survivors came out to survey the damage and rescue trapped survivors.

The sight made Delta King angry. He shook his fist at Bondage-Breaker. "You are my enemy forever," he shouted. "I will never let your people go."

But he had weakened when the brothers returned to the royal palace a few days later. "The sky holds more disasters if you do not listen to Bondage-Breaker."

That thought crumbled the king's resolve.

"No more," he begged. "The men may go if they leave the women and children."

"All must go!" said Brother.

"Then none will go."

The next morning General stretched out his shepherd's staff. A hot east wind blew off the great desert. It blew all day and all night. Then as the sun rose above the mountains of the dawn, the locusts were blown in—a thick wall of creatures crawled across the land, devouring anything that had been left by the storm. Shattered trees were stripped. Flattened crops were consumed. Every plant disappeared or was replaced by a woody skeleton. Little remained to eat except the insects themselves.

This time a grief-stricken Delta King stood before the brothers. He begged the brothers to stop the locusts.

"I have been hard-hearted and cruel to the People of the Promise. I will let them go."

General raised his shepherd's staff to the sky. A strong west wind arose. Locusts were blown out of the city and into the Sea of Reeds.

But Delta King wavered. "The people can't leave now. They must replant the fields."

General lifted his hand to the sky. The winds reversed. The east wind became a gale. Sand swirled into the air and darkened the sky. Clouds of grit and powder thickened as the wind grew stronger, shutting out the sunlight. The air was heavy and black and hot. It was hard to breathe. Sand blew into the eyes and mouth.

All this was horrible, but the intense blackness was even more frightening. For three days the sky was blotted out. People had only begun repairing after the hail. There was little protection from the wind and sand, and none from the darkness. No candles or lamps or even torches would remain lit. Frightened people huddled in total darkness, sweating in the stifling heat and gasping for breath. The weak or despairing died and were covered inside their own dwellings.

On the third day, though, the wind stopped. The sand fell to the ground. The sun could be seen once again. People rubbed their eyes and breathed the fresh air and marveled at the power of Bondage-Breaker.

A final time the brothers stood before Delta King.

"Bondage-Breaker has sent nine disasters. Three times he touched the river and three times he touched the land and three times he touched the sky. We can take no more. I will let your people go, but you must leave your animals. We need them to replenish our own livestock. We must have something to eat."

"You know we would perish without the animals for milk and meat. We must have them to begin a new life. We must take all of our animals."

"Never," spit Delta King with a snake-like hiss. "If you will not do it my way, you will never leave."

"It is not your way or our way that will save the Delta," replied General calmly. "It is Bondage-Breaker's way or death."

"Then it will be your death if I ever look upon either of you again!"

At the door, General turned to Delta King. "You need never see us

39

again. But you must answer to Bondage-Breaker. Nine times you have stood against him. One judgment remains. Then you will let the people go."

"Never!" cried the king.

The brothers walked through the palace courts once familiar to General, through the granite gates and through the City of the Sun. Not once did they look back.

Delta King watched them depart and wondered why he had not struck them down. Nobody had ever spoken or acted so insolently to him. A word would have been their destruction. So why had he not acted?

He didn't know.

CHAPTER 5

THE NIGHT OF NIGHTS

The People of the Pyramids were broken. They looked upon the People of the Promise with envy and respect and especially fear. Both peoples had experienced the flooding of the Wide River. Both had suffered from its deadly red algae and both had felt the the swarms of hungry mosquitoes after the invasion of frogs. But only the People of the Pyramids suffered through the biting flies and anthrax and burning abscesses and hail and locusts and the terrifying darkness.

But how could that be? Their slaves sat peacefully in their sunbaked brick houses untouched by disaster, while the favored people of the sun and river were ruined. Why had the gods cast them down and lifted up their slaves? It was incomprehensible. It sucked away at their confidence in those things they had believed in always.

Now they watched as the slave families built handcarts and herded their flocks together. The worksites were suddenly empty, but it seemed hard to restore order when an entire nation had failed to be at their tasks. And now even the cruelest drivers were afraid.

"What are you doing?" some people of the Delta asked the slaves.

"We are preparing to leave your land," came the answer.

"But Delta King will never let you go."

"In a few days he will beg us to go as quickly as we can."

"There will be another disaster? What will it be?"

"We do not know," said the slaves. "But it will be worse than the others."

The People of the Pyramids quaked.

The next morning the People of the Promise went to the houses of their masters and knocked boldly on their doors.

"We've come to ask for gifts."

"Why should we give gifts to our slaves?"

"Bondage-Breaker told us to go out and ask for gifts. When Bondage-Breaker speaks, it is dangerous not to listen. Don't you agree?"

The people nodded nervously. The taskmasters could not suffer another plague. "What gifts does the Bondage-Breaker wish us to give?" they asked their astonished visitors without hesitation.

"Gold and silver and clothing."

So the slaves moved from great poverty to great wealth in a single day. The astonished king could not believe the reports he was hearing about the slaves or the reports he was hearing about his own subjects.

The brothers were just as uncertain. "What should we do now?" they asked as they walked with Bondage-Breaker early the next day.

"Choose a lamb," said the wind. "Every family who wishes to follow me must choose a spotless male lamb. As the sun strikes the western horizon and the light fades, all the chosen lambs must be sacrificed. This must be done at the first twilight of the next full moon."

"Why then?" asked General.

"Because that will be the night of my passing," said the wind. "I will move through the land looking for those who won't listen to my voice."

"How will you know who listens and who doesn't?"

"I have special words for the People of the Promise: After they sacrifice their lamb, each family is to spill its blood and mark the frames of their doors with its redness. Mark both posts and the crosspiece with blood. When I move through the land I will see the blood and I will know you have listened."

"And where you do not see the blood?" asked General.

"The angel of death will claim the firstborn male. There will be great weeping in the land of the Delta. But I will pass by the houses that are marked with blood. All who listen and obey will be spared.

"This will be the night of nights.

"This will be the night of death.

"This will be the night on which I break bonds.

"Tell my people to mark their door frames and go inside and remain until dawn."

"What about Delta King?"

"Delta King will weep with the rest. He will call you and your brother to his palace just before the dawn. He will let my people go. Go quickly. Leave the land of the delta and don't look back."

"The people will sleep with their sandals on and their possessions packed."

Through the land went General and his brother. All of the slaves were instructed to choose a lamb for each family and at twilight on the appointed day to make their sacrifices. Every family was to mark their door frame with blood and remain inside their houses. They were to eat their final meal and be ready to set out. This was to be a special meal that would always be remembered on a night that would never be forgotten.

Those who were not descendants of Wrestler could come, if they joined in the sacrifice and placed the blood on their doors and agreed to walk with Bondage-Breaker. When they heard the wailing of their masters they would know the day of deliverance had come. All would journey as quickly as possible toward the gathering place. When everyone had gathered from the slave lands they would leave.

Delta King heard the spies' reports of all of this, but he did nothing. Uncertainty gnawed at his heart. He looked at his firstborn, a strong child who played near the foot of his throne during meetings of state. The other disasters had happened as General and Brother had declared.

Surely not this as well.

Each family gathered in their simple homes, quietly eating their meal of roasted lamb and dandelion salad and flat journey bread. The roasted lamb reminded them of the day Promise-Keeper accepted a ram in place of Merchant's son. The dandelion salad was bitter, representing the bitter years of toil and slavery at the hands of cruel taskmasters. The bread was flat because there had not been warning to let a special bread rise with yeast. So the flat bread represented haste. They would not have time to let their dough rise—for when the Bondage-Breaker says to go, one must go.

That midnight, a cloud crossed the full moon. The night went black. A chill entered the land and the People of the Promise huddled close in their little houses, waiting for Bondage-Breaker and the angel of death to pass. Every slave house was marked with blood, so Bondage-Breaker passed. But Bondage-Breaker stopped at each house that was not marked. The angel entered silently, peacefully, purposefully.

In each house the breath of a boy child or man grew shallow and ceased. From the tiniest infant to the most ancient father, every firstborn male became still. Wives reached out to find their husbands' bodies growing cold. Mothers ran to their sons, finding them limp and lifeless.

At first there was a single cry and a lamp was lit.

Within an hour a foreboding had swept entire cities.

Now screams and weeping burst from the land itself.

People of the Promise who lived near the houses of their masters heard the cries of pain as they huddled quietly together. They were spared, but what would Delta King do to them?

"I must see General and his brother now," demanded the king. "Go to their houses. Pull them from their beds. Do not waste a moment."

The messengers found General and his brother waiting quietly for them.

"My son is dead," wept the king when he saw them. "The son of the almighty Delta King, the heir to the world's greatest throne, my precious little boy. How could you do this?"

"We did nothing," said General. "You thought you were the almighty king who could defy Bondage-Breaker. He has reminded you that you are not."

"Take your people and go. Take whatever you want. Leave my kingdom as soon as the sun breaks above the mountains of the dawn."

"We will go," said General.

Delta King sat on his great throne with his body slumped forward and his head hung low. Sorrow clouded his tired eyes. He couldn't respond. His hard heart had shattered. Its pain ravaged him.

General felt pity for the king. Then he turned and walked through the audience hall.

"Stop," came a hollow voice.

"Yes?" asked General.

"Ask Bondage . . . Breaker . . . to bless me."

General walked back to the king. "Bondage-Breaker will bless anyone who listens to him and walks with him."

Uncomprehending, the exhausted king waved a finger of dismissal. He would think about the meaning of this sort of blessing another time.

Throughout the day the army of carts and ox-pulled wagons rolled on, continually joined by more and more people. General and Brother watched distant clouds of dust blur the horizon as thousands and thousands and thousands of refugees began their journey.

They had not comprehended the enormity of it.

How would anyone lead so many?

How would *they* lead so many?

Over the next days the People of the Promise grew to a swath of travelers as wide as a river and as long as the eye could see. They grew to two million strong, as they headed toward the eastern wilderness with the new day's sun shining bright in their faces.

The people felt the ecstasy of freedom. General and his brother felt the fear that they were not yet free of the lands of the changeable Delta King. Another three days, maybe four, and then across the Sea of Reeds. And what then? Could they cross that morass of swamp and shallow water with so many?

If they had known that Delta King's grief was turning at that moment to rage, they would have been even more fearful.

WITH AN ENEMY ON ONE SIDE
AND THE DEEP BLUE SEA
ON THE OTHER,
OPTIONS ARE AS LIMITED
AS FAITH.

CHAPTER 6

THE CROSSING

Follow me," said the wind, "and I will take you to a new land, a land with plenty of milk and honey."

"We will follow," replied General. "And we have brought the bones of Dreamer who long ago asked us to carry him back to the Valley of Apples."

A strong breeze blew from the west and collided with an east wind. The two twisted into a giant whirlwind that sucked sand from the desert floor until it became as thick as a cloud.

The people backed away in fear lest they be swallowed by the spinning wind.

"Don't be afraid," yelled General, and his words were relayed back. "Bondage-Breaker is in the cloud. He is our leader from this land of slavery."

The people cheered.

The whirlwind grew wide and tall as a small mountain. It moved east, spinning and twirling. General and his brother forgot their fears about either the Sea of Reeds or the people of the delta. Their eyes were fixed on the giant cloud. The pace increased as all were filled with excitement. All day they traveled, following the whirlwind. As the sun set at their backs, the cloud began to glow. The people stared ahead as the sand suspended in the wind shimmered with light. The darker the night became, the brighter the cloud shined until it blazed like phosphorescent fire.

The people stepped back and hid their faces when the voice of Bondage-Breaker himself burst from the cloud, loud enough for the end of the river of people to hear.

"I am Bondage-Breaker," said the fire, "and you are my people. I will guide you by day. I will protect you by night. Listen. Obey the words I tell General and Brother."

General stepped before the people. His clear voice carried far back, and others picked up the phrases so that all could hear.

"Remember our night of nights forever.

"Remember our final meal in the Land of Pyramids.

"Remember the passing of the angel of death.

"Tell your children and their children. At midnight our firstborn males were spared, so in gratitude let us set aside our firstborn sons for all time as special servants to Bondage-Breaker."

All the people agreed. That night they camped in the desert. All were exhausted, yet how could one sleep as Bondage-Breaker stood guard over them in a pillar of fire?

Normally the journey to the eastern border would take days. For two million people and ten million animals and thousands of fully packed wagons it took much longer. It was a massive undertaking to move so large a group. The desert landscape over which they passed made the journey harder. Yet with the whirlwind to guide and the blazing light to protect, the People of the Promise pushed on toward the Sea of Reeds. Here they stopped and stared at the waters before them. Freedom lay on the other side; they could see it, but how would they get there? The water seemed to be higher than normal. It was too deep to wade and too wide to swim.

"Why have you led us to this place?" they cried out to the whirlwind. "We are trapped. The only places of crossing lie to the north."

Bondage-Breaker was silent.

A serpent coiled on the warm sand, pleased by the people's plight. His eyes flickered as he looked to the west. Everything was going fine.

Two days before the snake had whispered in Delta King's ear, "How can you let these people go? Who will build your cities and palaces and pyramids? Now that your son has died, you need them more than ever. Without them how can you be great?"

The king had listened and now Shining One just waited, enjoying the scene and wondering why Bondage-Breaker had led them into such an impossible corner.

A rumble rolled across the desert and the ground shook. The people at the rear began to notice something far in the distance. Squinting in the bright sun they saw dark forms breaking the western horizon. As the sun sank lower the silhouettes of hundreds of the delta-king's elite war chariots raced toward them. Two tireless horses pulled each chariot which carried a driver and a warrior who flashed his sword in the fading light.

The people forgot the promises. They even forgot the great cloud at their front. They panicked. Trapped between the soldiers and the sea, they cried out to Bondage-Breaker. "Where have you led us? Delta King has changed his mind. His men will cut us down in revenge."

The wind spoke to General. "I promised I would guide and protect you. I always do as I say. By dawn you will be free and those who mean to do you harm will never bother you again. Tell my people to step into the sea and as they do, wave your shepherd's staff over the water. They will pass unharmed to freedom."

The whirlwind spun faster and lifted off the ground. The people quieted and nervously watched as the giant cloud passed over their heads and lowered to the ground just behind them. Like a barrier as solid as stone it stood strong between the chariots and the slaves. On the side of the soldiers was blackness, on the side of the slaves was a bright shining light.

The horses whinnied and pulled back until all the chariots were at a dead stop. The warriors lit torches and carefully approached the whirlwind. As they came close, their torches were blown out and they were pushed away by the mighty force of the wind. Again they tried, but the whirlwind only spun faster, pushing them away with an even greater force. The warriors mounted their horses and whipped them violently, but the animals would not go near the cloud. In frustration Delta King's army set up camp and waited through the night for the whirlwind to lift.

On the other side of the cloud, General asked the people to step into the sea and as they did, he waved his shepherd's staff over the water. The surface grew peaceful, so peaceful the people could see their reflections in the blue. Then something deep within the sea moved, sending ripples out in all directions. The ripples grew larger until all the water before them moved back and forth in a gentle roll. Minutes passed and the movement escalated into a violent rocking that stirred the sea into huge surges and swells. These surges and swells crashed and collided, forcing water high into the air. Then the earth shuddered and the wheels of time seemed to stop. The waves froze in place, creating two vertical walls of water with a wide, dry way in between.

The people stared in amazement until General ordered them quickly forward. All night long the escaping slaves moved their wagons and flocks through the sea bed on dry sand. Finally the last people reached the eastern bank. Day was breaking, and the solid cloud which stopped Delta King's warriors lifted. The men were ordered into their chariots. They mounted their horses and rushed to the Sea of Reeds. Here they stopped, perplexed by the path cut between two walls of water. It seemed impossible, but it was unmistakably there. And it was the only way across. A hard path had even been worn by footprints and wooden wheels. So the drivers whipped their horses and the chariots sped into the sea. About halfway across, the weight of the chariots with their heavy bronze armor dug into the sand. The horses sweated and snorted as they tried to keep what they pulled from getting stuck. But each vehicle made deeper ruts for those behind it and soon they all bogged down. The drivers frantically whipped their horses even harder, the animals bolted and jerked, breaking the chariots' axles. The wheels fell off and everything dragged to a stop. The warriors stepped from their vehicles. They sank to their knees in mud. The horses broke free and charged aimlessly about, churning the mud even more. Those in command shouted meaningless orders and cursed Delta King.

Most of the People of the Promise had moved on as fast as they could. But the last of their column saw this chaos behind them and thanked Bondage-Breaker for their freedom. General's brother urged the people on. General stood alone on the bank, watching the judgment of Bondage-Breaker unfold. Once he had commanded chariots such as these. Now he waved his shepherd's staff over the sea and the walls broke. Water crashed down, racing toward the meeting point where the soldiers stood frozen in terror. The waters slammed onto them at once, swallowing every warrior and every chariot and every animal.

No one now pursued the People of the Promise. No one was even alive to tell Delta King the fate of his finest chariot warriors and strongest horses.

As the early morning sun sparkled on the once again peaceful sea, General called out to his people. "Bondage-Breaker has broken our bonds. He has set us free."

Two million cheers arose. Even children joined in, not all that sure what everyone was so happy about. Minutes later the great assembly that stretched into the distance quieted. General continued:

"He has guided and protected us.

"He is infinite and eternal and all-powerful.

"He is Garden-Maker and Promise-Keeper and Bondage-Breaker."

There was no more travel that day. An immense city formed around the rich plain by the Sea of Reeds. An impromptu festival came together in the middle. Families were reunited. People laughed and then wept. Stories of the past were shared of Builder and Land Baron and Wrestler.

Overwhelming joy filled their hearts as they hugged and congratulated each other. Throughout the great camp people broke into song. Sometimes they sang together. Sometimes they sang in groups. Sometimes it was beautiful and moving. Sometimes it didn't sound so good. But no one cared. At the very center of this throng, a great crowd clapped as General's sister started to dance with a tambourine. Horns and lyres and cymbals played with passion. People grabbed each others' hands and the entire camp joined the dance.

Through the heat of the day and into the cool of the evening, the festival continued with singing and celebrating. The whirlwind stood close and Bondage-Breaker smiled.

As night settled on the dance of freedom the broken bodies of warriors washed up on the eastern shore. Between the corpses slithered the ancient serpent, hissing obscenities at the flame of the one above all.

> TOO MANY COMPLAINTS
> BLIND ONE TO ALL THAT IS
> GOOD AND POSITIVE IN LIFE.

CHAPTER 7

THE COMPLAINTS

By the next day much weaponry and armor had washed up onto the shore. General ordered all to be gathered. At some point the people would have to be an army. Then he gathered all the clan leaders before him.

"Before us is the way of the wilderness," said General. "Obstacles lie between us and our land. There will be days of little food and water. But if we follow Bondage-Breaker, he will meet our needs. There will be battles with fierce armies who resist the one beyond the sky. But we will prevail."

"Shepherds and brick makers and pyramid builders cannot fight in battle," said the grumblers.

"Put on the armor Bondage-Breaker provides," said General.

"Sharpen the swords he gives.

"Face each enemy with confidence—and Bondage-Breaker will do the rest."

The People of the Promise followed the cloud south into a dry, stony land of only scattered brush. For three long days the people walked with no sign of water. After two days their supply ran out; on the third day their throats were parched. But late that afternoon, those in front of the column saw palm trees on the horizon.

It was no trick of the heat, but real trees with a spring bubbling into a sparkling pool. Excitement spread through the crowd and hope brightened every eye. Those closest rushed forward, but the first to reach the pool spit and gagged. The water was bitter and brackish—so salty that those who drank were more desperate than ever. The animals had to be driven back, for too much of this water would kill.

"We've been tricked," cried a voice.

"We still have no drinkable water," said another.

"Look how weak we are," a woman yelled. "Look at our dying children."

"Bondage-Breaker has led us astray, and we are going to die!" The wail spread throughout the camp and no one heard General call to them: "If Bondage-Breaker can divide a sea, he can sweeten a spring."

He looked to the wind. "What would you have me do?"

The wind whispered in his ear, and he listened. He went to a nearby barberry bush and cut off a limb and threw it in the spring. Then he drank from the pool, now sweet and refreshing.

It took many hours, but the thirst of all was quenched. By morning even the animals were satisfied.

Yet another day's journey south was a much larger oasis with twelve springs of sweet, flowing water. Here the people could fill their water containers. They could take their first true rest since the night of nights. They could laugh in the shade of scattered palms and jujube trees. Other travelers who stopped at the oasis wondered at the people who filled the sands surrounding the springs. From these travelers General heard that a dangerous desert tribe had noticed their approach. General knew of all the wilderness peoples. This was the worst and they would not easily be discouraged even by so large a company.

There were several large nomadic bands of these people of the desert and all were fearless fighters. All followed Shining One. When not killing each other, they joined in cruel raids on villages or caravans or anyone who might hold wealth. They stalked their prey and watched and waited. Already they had taken stragglers from the rear of the descendants of Wrestler. These prisoners told their stories under torture, then felt the slicing knife across their throats. What they told was unbelievable, but so was the immense and eerie cloud of dust that was there for all to see.

The nomads also knew that the strange people had wealth. They carried abundant gold and silver. It was enough to risk a whirlwind to find.

A rear guard now watched to protect the slower travelers. General knew well, however, that he was not yet ready to face an army of bandits.

A full cycle of the moon had passed since the night of nights. The People of the Promise entered a land more empty and desolate than anything they had yet seen.

"I hate it here. It's too hot."

"We've run out of food. My children are weak and dying."

"We are all going to starve to death."

"Quiet!" yelled General before the assembly. "If Bondage-Breaker can sweeten a bitter spring, he can feed his people."

General looked to the wind. "What would you have me do?" The wind whispered its reply and General stood before the people.

"Bondage-Breaker will provide meat at twilight and bread at dawn. Eat your fill and look beyond the sky. If you walk with Bondage-Breaker he will meet your needs."

That evening as the light turned dim General spread his people across the desert. Silently they stared at the flat features that blended with the darkening sky. Then came the sound of distant thunder made by the beating of countless wings—steady and rhythmic and growing louder. With a flash the whirlwind burst into flame and the desert glowed. The sky was now alive with small brown quail. The flock of millions was exhausted after a long migration toward the headwaters of the Wide River.

Tired quail flew into their outstretched hands and were thrown into woven baskets. The people ate heartily, and meat was left that could be dried in the hot desert sun.

Early in the morning as General walked with Bondage-Breaker, a heavy white dew fell over the land. Slowly awakening people peered from their tents, thinking this sight was a dream. The desert floor was covered with a thin layer of white that crunched underfoot, making footprints.

"Gather it quickly," said General, "and eat it before it melts with the sun."

The people bent down and collected the white frost. It tasted like bread—thick and grainy and sweet. Good.

"Enjoy your morning bread," said Bondage-Breaker to General. "Six dawns a week will I provide this bread for my people. On the sixth morning gather enough for the seventh day. There will be no bread on that morning. Until you enter the land of plenty, I will provide you with bread."

As the people wandered toward the desert mountains, six out of seven dawns were white.

Bondage-Breaker had fulfilled his promise. General stood once more at that mountain with the descendants of Wrestler. But it wasn't as General had hoped. Water had run short again. Tempers were high.

"We're so thirsty."

"Give us water."

"Look what you've done to us; look at our children!"

A mob of complainers picked up stones and approached General with menace. "He doesn't deserve to live after everything he's put us through."

"You have not followed me to this place," yelled General. "You have followed Bondage-Breaker. If you want to throw stones, throw them at him. He has provided quail in the night and bread in the morning. Don't you think he can give you water?"

General walked over to a large outcropping of rock on the side of the mountain. Everybody's eyes were fixed on him. He lifted his shepherd's staff above his head and brought it down hard on the rock.

The mountain shuddered.

The people stepped back.

The rock split apart and a torrent gushed.

Every container was brought and filled while children drank. Water collected in a natural rock basin and overflowed in cascading rivulets into a larger natural rock pool. Through the day and into the night, the stream showed no sign of slowing.

"Forgive our complaints," the leaders of the clans told General. "Bondage-Breaker has provided our every need. He is our guide and protector. He has guided us and protected us well. We have no need to worry. He is infinite and eternal and all-powerful."

General reminded his people of the lesson of the rainbow: "He is always close and he will always care."

The people camped here many days, enjoying the cool, clear water that flowed from a subterranean source. But as the people relaxed a new danger crept in with the darkness. The warrior band, with speed and ruthlessness, raided outlying groups of people. Screams were heard. Men who fought back were cut down. Others disappeared, as did precious animals. Tents were torched.

The people of the desert had to be stopped. General searched for a suitable warrior to lead. Many pointed out a young man from a prominent family who showed shrewdness and courage. General called him to his tent.

"Choose the strongest and bravest. I can teach you military tactics, but that will have to wait. Tomorrow you go to battle."

The young man sent runners through the camp. Everything that could be used as a weapon was sharpened and cleaned and brought to the new commander. He recruited the strongest. Scouts came and went with news of the raiders' camp. At dawn a little army set out to war. On a hill overlooking the enemy camp General watched the first charge by the People of the Promise. For the first time sword struck sword. Force collided with force and blood spilled and warriors died.

The young man moved quickly and with cunning. He inspired confidence. The excited General lifted his shepherd's staff with both hands over his head. From the battlefield the army saw General's silhouette against the bright sky. As long as the staff was raised, the raiders fell back before the descendants of Wrestler. But as General's arms grew weary and sank, the enemy took courage. General's brother and his sister's husband saw what was happening. They rushed to his side. One stood on his right. One stood at his left. They lifted his arms high.

That night the people praised Bondage-Breaker.

Wounds were dressed and the fallen mourned.

A wise young commander was honored.

General walked alone to the mountain he knew so well. In his arms was a spotless newborn lamb. He built an altar, and watched the sweet smoke of his sacrifice curl upward.

"You are our victory," he said.

"You are my people," said the wind. "I will show you more victories."

"We will follow."

CHAPTER 8

THE MOUNTAIN

In three days a great trumpet will shake the mountain."

"We will listen," said the people.

"When you hear and feel my call, gather before me."

"We will gather."

A thick cloud shrouded the peak that third morning. Thunder rumbled and bolts zigzagged to the ground. Parents grabbed children and hurried toward shelter.

Then they stopped.

"Did you hear?"

Thunder faded to silence. A single, clear note settled upon them, gentle and melodic. Though it was not loud, the very rocks of the mountain began to shake with it.

The people turned toward the thick cloud covering the mountain. The trumpet now made them tremble with its piercing strength. If one sound could be said to embody all sounds and all emotions perfectly, such was this note.

They thrilled at the resonance of power and excitement.

They savored the sense of purity and beauty.

They saw the shape of infinity and eternity.

The transfixing sound ceased. Without a word of question all moved toward the open plain by the great peak. General waited there, looking up into the dark cloud, until a great multitude stood with him, shoulder to shoulder:

elders on crutches;

swaddled infants;

children perched on parent shoulders.

A new note split the air, painful, so that hands covered ears. "Come close to the mountain," shouted General. "Stand close, but do not step onto its rocky base or you will die." Fire exploded in the midst of the cloud to punctuate the warning. Sparks showered the rocks and dark smoke billowed from crevices. Then all hushed once more.

As smoke mingled with vapors the sun seemed ready to extinguish its blaze at the approach of Bondage-Breaker. Only the fire of mountain and cloud illuminated the world.

The voice when it came was not loud so much as soul-shattering. No heralds need repeat these words for those behind.

"I live beyond the sky, but I am always close and I will always care.

"Hear my ten words; sing them; obey them. You will live as my people with these words on your tongues and in your hearts. Dance them with your lives and be my chorus throughout the blue planet. Those who allow these notes to fail sink into slavery."

"We will listen. We will follow," said General. *Were their ears and hearts open? Would they sing these words?* General wondered.

"COMMIT!"

The voice echoed about the mountain and faded. But deep inside the echoed refrain bounced about the heartwalls— *"Commit all your mind and heart and will to me."*

"WALK!"

The word seemed etched into the fabric of the land. "Walk with me, so you will not be distracted by Shining One."

"DEFEND!"

Bondage-Breaker had defended them. "Defend my honor and reputation while you rescue my little ones from Shining One."

"REST!"

Here was rest beyond body. "Recline in me; then you will see garden paths for walking by my side."

"HONOR!"

Now the melody changed to an earthy key. "Honor all whom I send to direct your lives."

"LOVE!"

New colors and dimensions burst into being: "Love summarizes all. Desire good and peace and joy for others."

"CLEAVE!"

Husbands and wives clasped hands at the hymn of unity. "Hold one another close and avoid all that divides you. Be lovers who hate walls."

"RESPECT!"

The word was caroled in heroic splendor. "Respect life and so respect Garden-Maker. Respect all that belongs to another."

"TRUTH-TELL!"

A somber dirge tolled the pain of deceits that dishonor. "Let your words and actions throw open large windows of candor."

"DELIGHT!"

"Delight in all I give," hummed the lay of satisfaction in Bondage-Breaker, "and do not long for what belongs to another."

"Hear my words," proclaimed Bondage-Breaker. "Follow."

"Will you listen and follow his ways?" asked General. "He has more to teach."

"We will listen, . . . but the voice . . . !" gasped the leaders of the people. "His voice will unmake us."

"I will go up and hear his voice for you."

General cut two flat stones from the base of the mountain, stones like those on which rulers carve their profoundest thoughts. He cut the stones from the place where he had tended his flock, had seen fire on the mountain. Strapping the stones to his back, he adjusted their weight.

Now he would climb as he had on that night. He would return to where the bush burned and was not consumed. Now he would struggle under the weight of stone and of a stone-hearted people. But it was bearable, for Bondage-Breaker walked with him on the mountain path, lifting his burdens. General felt his old limbs become young, and vigor coursed his muscles. His heart skipped ahead of his steps. Joy crowded his heart.

The people saw only an ancient man fading into the cloud. They felt alone without his familiar presence and drifted away in silence.

Days passed.

In weeks General did not return. Through a moon cycle the mysterious mountain remained swathed in vapor. Watchers waited, but the sullen stone giant hid its secrets.

"The fool took no food or water."

"He is dead by now."

"He went mad from hearing the voice."

"General was not afraid to climb," said Brother. "He knew what waited on the summit. Bondage-Breaker is always close and always cares. Give him another week."

The people waited. And the deadline passed.

Now Brother was shaken. He stood at the edge of the silent mountain, peering upward for something—anything. Tears crossed the deep wrinkles of his windblown face. What had gone wrong? This wasn't how it should end.

"That's Bondage-Breaker for you," hissed a voice. "In the end he goes his way. He led you here, but he's lost interest. He discarded General."

"It is not true!" cried Brother, though his confidence didn't reach the volume of his denial.

A snake sunned lazily by a huge boulder. "You yourself set the time-limit. Now face the truth," the serpent started to slither off, then looked back. "It's really too bad," he said. "You could survive, but you will keep looking up there until it is too late." Now the snake was disappearing beneath the rock.

"Wait!" shouted Brother. "How can we survive if General's dead and Bondage-Breaker has abandoned us?"

Piercing eyes like pools of night peeked from under the rock. "I have the power. Follow me."

"How . . . how would we follow you?" breathed Brother, taken by the soft voice of reason.

"Build me an image like the ones in the Land of Pyramids. You know the craft of the priests. Then bow before the image and listen to my words."

"Bow before you?" The matter would have ended there, for Brother knew this was both evil and ridiculous. But as he returned to camp he was surrounded by leaders of the clans.

"We have all dreamed the same tragic and wondrous message," they said. "A great serpent has revealed to us the death of General. He told us to look to you, that you will make us a golden calf who will lead us to safety. We will return to Egypt, where Delta King is beaten and will accept us as equals, not slaves."

Brother sat on a rock, so tired.

"This is wrong," he said at last, "but I don't know what else to do."

"We have collected gold jewelry. It is waiting."

Brother worked sadly and slowly and hoping more than ever for General's return. He carved the shape of a calf from wood. He encased it in a sand mixture that hardened as it dried. With care he cut it open, removed the carving and reclosed the mold.

Hotter and hotter the fire was stoked. The pot glowed. The pieces inside became soft and pliable and thick—glowing soup. Now it was liquid and he poured it into the mold. The next day the mold was broken away, and the excess trimmed. Cleaned and buffed, the work of art gleamed in the sun.

Time had run out.

"You have the golden calf; you don't need Bondage-Breaker," hissed the snake. "The calf will defeat your enemies and lead you to the land of blessing and peace."

"We will listen," said the people.

"We will follow."

Brother built a stone altar before the golden calf. At daybreak a hundred spotless newborn lambs bled on the altar before the sculpture.

On the mountain, Bondage-Breaker stopped teaching.

"You have grown quiet," said General.

"Your people have turned their backs on this mountain. They go the way of Shining One."

No one saw General emerge from the mist, in his arms the stone tablets with five words written by the finger of Bondage-Breaker on either side. General watched and listened to the vulgar crowd. They drank much wine and danced in a wild, chaotic frenzy. Their obscenities cursed the work of Garden-Maker and the promises of Promise-Keeper and the mighty acts of Bondage-Breaker. They did not see the serpent wrap around the neck of the golden calf, but he grew larger and larger.

General ignored the snake wrapped around the neck of the sculpture. Only the snake had watched the mountain. He alone saw General's approach.

"What have you done?" It was an anguished scream.

"General has returned."

Word spread and the revelers grew silent.

He stood above them on a rock outcropping, weeping. Some who saw him felt unclothed and dirty. Others were annoyed: He was spoiling their celebration. None voiced this complaint, though. He stood there shaking with fury. With eyes blazing he raised the two record stones above his head.

He threw them at the altar where they shattered.

"Is this absurd scrap of metal now your master?"

He had jumped to the outcropping on which the calf rested. It tipped and fell and shattered among shards of the record stones in the altar fire. The fire flared, white hot, until the statue melted away to leave golden puddles in the dirt.

Brother lay prostrate at the feet of General.

"You *know* Bondage-Breaker. Are you now his betrayer?" asked General. "How could you lead our people to Shining One?"

"I listened to Shining One out of doubt. I followed out of fear. I stopped watching and took my eyes from the mountain."

General softened. "You are a traitor with no right to ask for mercy." He turned and shouted, "All of you are traitors. But Bondage-Breaker loves to forgive those who have no right to ask."

"Turn from Shining One.

"Listen again.

"Follow once more."

Those who returned to Bondage-Breaker were humbled. So easily they had been distracted. The rest stubbornly refused to return and would soon come to regret their foolishness.

A GENEROUS HEART
STRETCHES BEYOND ITSELF,
A SELFISH HEART RARELY REACHES
BEYOND ITS OWN FINGERTIPS.

CHAPTER 9

THE SPECIAL PLACE

I want to know you better."

General made his plea as he walked through the dawn with Bondage-Breaker.

"Whenever you move close to me, I will move close to you," said Bondage-Breaker.

"I know, but I have never truly seen you. Show me your face."

"You have seen my fire.

"You have heard my voice.

"You have felt my breath."

"Yes, and it is enough to sustain me. Yet, I long for more."

"If you look long at the sun you will become blind. My face is many times brighter. If you look into my eyes their perfection would un-make you."

"Oh, that I might be unmade as I look on your face."

"You will someday know me as I am. But you must walk yet awhile in the dimness of your world. Then I will invite you to stand alongside Merchant and Wrestler in my presence."

"Is there nothing I can see of the reality?"

"Return to the mountain, and you will see what you are able. Bring record stones, as before, and I will again write my ten words."

Early the next morning, before the sun topped the mountains, General walked into the thick black cloud. Instead of darkness he saw completion and contentment.

Again on pieces of stone Bondage-Breaker wrote the words. He told more of his ways. The student listened with unstopped ears and ate uncommon food and rested unclouded sleep.

After forty days General felt closer to Bondage-Breaker than ever before. "You have humbled me indeed. You have shown more of your presence than any on the blue planet have known."

General stood and took up his shepherd's staff and the record stones. He tied on his sandals by the plateau of rock. But something here was not the same. The sheer face of the mountain was now broken by a fissure. This narrow corridor into the darkness had not been there before.

"You have grown enough to see yourself as you are. So you have grown enough to see more of me. Go into the mountain. I will pass by and you will see my silhouette."

Without hesitation he removed his shoes. He entered the cave and felt his way deeper until the opening was a small dot of light. In the darkness he came to a small stone step at the base of a wall. There he knelt.

Suddenly the tunnel was a blazing blur of burning light. Was this the dark of Bondage-Breaker's silhouette? He seemed adrift in time. He saw the darkest, saddest days of life on the blue planet:

War and hatred,
pain and anarchy,
every possible evil from the heart of Shining One.

Why were these images coming out of the light? When it seemed he could take in no more light nor watch more suffering the haze was lifted from his mind. He gasped at the brilliance and beauty and purity. He searched for words but could find none. All he saw was so far beyond the limits of language that he was left stunned and speechless. He stepped back and saw light overcome darkness. He watched evil submit.

The worst hopelessness became the greatest triumph.

Overwhelming trials led to miraculous interventions. Horrific misery was eclipsed by unending strength and comfort. Each event could be seen now as a silver stepping-stone in a perfect plan. The stones merged into a translucent highway, and the dark silhouette melted into an exquisite rainbow.

The shaft grew dark once more.

It took minutes to adjust to the dimness and find a way toward the opening.

In a daze General collected his belongings and wandered down the mountain. Perhaps later he could make some sense of what he had seen and heard and felt. Not yet. It was too much. He said little about it when he reached the camp. What could be said?

The people ran when he approached. Children cried. Their parents fell to their knees and buried their heads in their hands.

"What is wrong?" asked General.

"Please, sir, hide your face from us. You have the face of Bondage-Breaker himself."

General set down the record stones and walked to the pool of water. His face was brighter than the sun. His reflection burned his own eyes, for he knew that he still glowed with the light of the silhouette. For a time he would have to cover his face from the people though all too soon its brilliance would fade.

"Tell us what you have learned from Bondage-Breaker."

"If you move close to Bondage-Breaker," summarized General, "he will move close to you."

On the mountain the thick black cloud had lifted. The smoke and sparks had disappeared. The steep rocky profile of the great mountain was framed by blue sky.

"Where has Bondage-Breaker gone?" everyone wondered.

"He is always close, and he always cares," said General.

"Sometimes he's in a fire and sometimes in a whirlwind and sometimes in a thick, black cloud, but he is always close."

"Should we build a home for Bondage-Breaker?" asked the people when General gathered them together. "He doesn't live in sculptures or places. How can we build a home for one who lives beyond the sky and holds the stars in his hands?"

"He doesn't *need* a house," General answered. "But he wants a Special Place for meeting with us. It is for us the house must be built. And he will set it apart to himself. On the mountain he told me how to build his home. It will not be easy."

"What shall we do?"

"Bring gold and silver given by the People of the Pyramids.

"Prepare copper and cloth, hardwood and hides.

"Find the best incense and oil."

So the people brought what was needed to the center of camp. They sorted through their treasures and brought until more had been given than was needed.

Early the next morning hundreds of workmen gathered. Some were appointed—master artists and craftsmen, designers and metalsmiths, carpenters and weavers. They crowded with others who wanted to take part in the center of camp with their tools—many more than could possibly be used at one time. In six cycles of the moon they took great care to complete and furnish a home for Bondage-Breaker according to the plan.

It was still a tent and could be taken apart and moved with the people. But such a tent—so striking in beauty and simplicity. Its sides were richly woven. Its flat roof measured fifteen paces wide and forty-five paces long. It was taller than three men standing on each others' shoulders. A hundred silver braces held a wooden frame. From it hung a curtain of the thickest and finest linen, dyed blue and purple and scarlet while embroidered with figures of magnificent angels.

Inside were two rooms separated by a single linen curtain. Here the curtain hooks were gold rather than silver, for the larger room was the Hallowed Chamber; in it was a golden table and a golden candelabra and a golden stand on which incense was to be burned.

The smaller room was dark, for it was the Most Hallowed Chamber. Here Bondage-Breaker would dwell. This room was empty, but for a wooden chest, covered inside and out with purest gold. On its lid two golden angels faced one another with outstretched wings. This was the ark of mystery. It enclosed the stones written on with the finger of the one above all.

A large enclosed courtyard surrounded the tent. It opened toward the mountains of the dawn. Inside this was a large copper altar for sacrifices to Bondage-Breaker. In the courtyard was a copper water basin where all who entered the Special Place could wash themselves clean.

On the day it was finished, the whirlwind that had led the people from the Land of Pyramids moved to the center of the camp. It lifted and spun over the Special Place. Then in a burst of thunder and a flash of lightning, the Bondage-Breaker entered the Most Hallowed Chamber. The Special Place glowed and all the people lay face down to honor the one above all.

General called his brother.

"Bondage-Breaker has set apart you and your four sons to maintain the Special Place and make the sacrifices." Brother and his four sons were declared keepers of the Special Place. Brother sacrificed a spotless ram on the copper altar and looked out at the people:

"May he who is above all things bless and keep you.

"May he guide and protect you as you follow him.

"May he break every bond and give you peace."

The two brothers washed their hands in the copper water basin and entered the Hallowed Chamber. Hours passed and the people waited. The sun set and still the people waited. When they reappeared the whirlwind above the Most Hallowed Chamber started to glow. It grew brighter and brighter until it was as the sun. The people covered their eyes and turned their faces.

Suddenly flames shot from the whirlwind, throwing white-hot sparks into the courtyard surrounding the Special Place. The flames slammed into the copper altar and exploded into a puff of smoke. When the air cleared, the body of the ram had been consumed and all that was left was a layer of red glowing coals. The people shouted for joy and fell face-down to the ground.

Brother had two humble sons and two proud sons. When the humble sons saw the flames of the Bondage-Breaker they fell face-down with the people. But the proud sons kept their faces upward. They were chosen, weren't they. Theirs was the right to approach Bondage-Breaker, for they were his favorites.

When the sons lit the incense on the golden incense stand, the humble sons took the coals from the copper altar and respectfully entered the Hallowed Chamber. They thanked Bondage-Breaker for allowing them to be keepers of the Special Place.

But the proud sons drank too much wine, and they did not light their incense with the coals Bondage-Breaker had left for them. Fire was fire. They started their own fire and entered the Hallowed Chamber with vulgar laughter and high heads. They tripped over the golden candelabra and swore when it crashed to the ground, throwing the room into darkness.

The ground under the Special Place rumbled and quaked. The whirlwind lowered into the Most Hallowed Chamber and the curtain that separated the two rooms stirred. The whirlwind spun faster and the proud sons heard a mournful howl. They pulled aside the curtain and peered into the blackness. The ark began to glow, bathing the room in blood-red light. The wind spun at a dizzying speed atop the ark of mystery between the golden angels.

"Why do you not listen to my words?" boomed the voice of Bondage-Breaker.

The proud sons turned to flee, but flames burst from the whirlwind. Their screams were cut off; their bodies were engulfed. General ran to the Special Place. Yet all he saw were the charred remains of rebellion. He shook his head and ordered the bodies to be carried away to a lonely place outside the camp.

General sadly regarded Brother and his two humble sons. It was natural that they grieved, but it was not right.

"Do not mourn the arrogant, who dismiss Bondage-Breaker's commands. They took lightly the one who lives beyond the sky and holds the stars in his hands. He has stooped to live in this dwelling place. But stooping makes him no less, but rather more. Only Brother has leave to enter that room and live."

So Brother put aside his brokenness and when the time was right, he prepared himself and respectfully parted the curtain. The whirlwind spun between the two angels on the ark of mystery. Brother lowered his head and honored Bondage-Breaker. The ark glowed and Brother stepped back. Would he too be condemned and consumed, for he was also a lawbreaker?

But there was no burst of flames.

"Those who listen to my words and follow my ways have nothing to fear," whispered the whirlwind.

BURDENS THAT CRUSH ONE
CAN BE EASILY SHOULDERED
BY MANY.

CHAPTER 10

THE EDGE

Everyone got up from his mats or stopped the early morning gathering of bread. A blast from twin trumpets echoed through the camp. A sea of people turned toward the Special Place. Each strained for a look at what was happening. The two remaining sons of Brother stood in the early morning light with silver trumpets to their lips. The people were silent, and the whirlwind spun above the Special Place. It sparkled in the yellow glow of dawn and lifted high into the air. Then the whirlwind touched down with a swirl of sand to the north.

"It is time to follow Bondage-Breaker," cried out General. Heralds shouted the commands back through the camp.

The people burst into activity, for much had to be done. Tents had to be taken down, wagons and carts loaded, flocks gathered from sparse pasture miles away. Brother and his two sons organized the careful packing of the Hallowed Chamber and the Most Hallowed Chamber. For eleven cycles of the moon the people had camped in the shadow of the mountain. Much had changed.

Now it was time to move.

The whirlwind led north, and they followed.

The ark of mystery was carried before all.

General scanned the wilderness and called out, "Those who follow Shining One should flee. Bondage-Breaker is passing through the land."

The people cheered and dust from four million sandals lifted a brown cloud above the desert.

The People of the Promise traveled north under a scorching red sun. They grew tired and sweaty and thirsty. They complained about the heat and food and about General and about Bondage-Breaker.

In the late afternoon of the third day, the complaints turned bitter. The words became caustic and cutting and cruel. The people were faithless for they had forgotten the source of good. The more they grumbled, the faster the whirlwind spun, and the more it glowed.

Now it blazed brighter than the setting sun. Sparks flashed through the air and crashed into the desert. Dry scrub brush and juniper burst into flames. A strong west wind fanned the flames.

The people threw sand on the flames. They beat the burning brush with wet woolen blankets. Animals scattered and children cried as the fires resisted control. The desert winds blew stronger and the flames lit the night sky. Smoke engulfed the camp and many ran into the desert.

"Help us!" they cried to General.

"Only Bondage-Breaker can help you, for this is his judgment."

"Ask him to save us. If the fire continues, all we have will be destroyed."

"You will still have Bondage-Breaker."

"But our lives will be in ashes."

"They already are."

General approached the spinning fire of the whirlwind. He moved so close the people thought it would consume him. He reached out and whispered, "Please be patient with your people. We are selfish and immature, but we wish to follow you."

The winds stopped and a drop of water wet his face. A rare desert rain cloud covered the camp and the burning land. A moment before the sky had been star-filled. Now drops fell faster. The sprinkle became a shower and then a downpour. The wildfires were extinguished. Soot was washed from each person who stood outside and pointed a blackened face upward. There was even drinking water.

The next morning relieved people went out to collect handfuls of bread. But Shining One crawled from beneath a scorched juniper bush to stir their discontent.

"How boring," hissed the snake. "Back in the Land of Pyramids you had good food. You had fish and fowl, fruit and vegetables. Here all you have is this so-called bread."

Murmurs of discontent turned into whines. Passing a tent, General heard what the people said inside: "Shining One is right. We had it better in the Land of Pyramids."

General hung his head and walked on. In the next tent he heard,

"We're tired of bread. Why can't we have meat?" Throughout the camp the grumbling was heard.

"We want meat."

"Bondage-Breaker doesn't understand our needs."

"General doesn't care."

Tears welled in his eyes. He sighed painfully and collapsed to the ground in the courtyard of the Special Place. He buried his face in his hands and wept in deep, heaving sobs. The whirlwind burned. "My people are stubborn," said Bondage-Breaker as sparks shot from the heart of the whirlwind. "Though flames touched the edge of their camp, they still did not learn."

"They are your people, not mine. Why didn't you leave me in the wilderness with my sheep? They are selfish and immature and impossible to satisfy. End my life. Stop my heart. Strike me with fire. Do anything so that I can find peace."

"Remember the mountain. Have you forgotten that I am peace? Even when life is disordered and unjust and harsh, my way is serenity.

"Remember before you came to the mountain. You were weary and your father-in-law told you not to bear the burden of leadership alone. You chose faithful and honest leaders to help shoulder the burden, and you had rest. Now bring the best of those leaders to the Special Place. I will touch their hearts. It is time for them to help you shoulder this burden as well."

"But the people demand meat."

"It is dangerous to make demands," said Bondage-Breaker. "Tomorrow they will have what they demand until they are sick of the sight and smell and taste of it."

A west wind blew the quail into camp as it had the previous spring, only now there were many more. The small brown birds beat their wings to stay aloft, but they were so exhausted that they were in reach even of children. Hungrily the entire camp went out to catch the quail, throwing them into large woven baskets. All that day and all the next day the piles of birds grew. There was more than could be eaten or dried. The dead birds began to spoil. Most ate meat that had gone bad, until sick people were everywhere. A putrid odor permeated the camp. Women dug holes to bury the remaining quail. Men dug graves for the dead.

The people moved ever farther north. Special bread covered the ground six out of seven mornings, and they were satisfied. Leaders now helped

General, counselors whose hearts were lifted and turned toward Bondage-Breaker. A cycle of the moon passed; then another.

Then danger approached from a new and totally unexpected direction. The General's sister, always a source of strength, began to whisper in small gatherings as one who had been with Shining One.

"I worry about General. He is worn out, and too emotional to handle the responsibility."

"But now other leaders stand alongside him," responded some.

"It isn't enough, for he has lost touch with the People of the Promise. He who became a man in the palace of Delta King has never understood we who were slaves. He left us all for forty summers and married an outsider."

"You are right. She doesn't know our ways."

"She doesn't look like us."

"They are both outsiders."

She put up her hands for quiet. "General received the ten words and his face glowed for a time. That was a blessing," she said. "But does Bondage-Breaker speak *only* to him? The one beyond the sky gave me a song to sing after we passed through the Sea of Reeds."

"Bondage-Breaker gave me words to speak before Delta King," added Brother. He was still heavy in heart because of the death of his sons, and perhaps a little bitter. General had not allowed him to grieve.

"So," said the sister, "how can we get the people to recognize what we've done? After all, he wouldn't even be alive if we hadn't hid his basket in the marshes."

"He is the leader chosen by Bondage-Breaker," argued Brother.

"He needs rest, needs time alone. If he became sick or had a broken bone, it would only limit him for a week or two. But that would give the people time to see that we too are chosen by Bondage-Breaker and are as important as General."

"I won't have anything to do with . . . ."

The sudden appearance of General abruptly ended the conversation. General ignored the awkwardness and put his arms around his siblings. "Bondage-Breaker wants to meet us at the Special Place."

"Why?" asked the sister in alarm.

"I don't know," said General. "But when Bondage-Breaker speaks, it is best to listen."

The three went to the Special Place and a wisp of wind whirled around at its entrance. "Brother and Sister, step forward," ordered the wind. They obeyed. "I speak to all who walk with me, but some are willing to walk longer and follow me farther. This is true of General. He teaches my words and directs the people to my ways. He has seen my silhouette and I have called him to lead. So why do the two of you speak disrespectfully of my faithful servant?"

Brother fell to his knees and cried, "We were wrong. I am sorry."

"The one who is infinite and eternal and all-powerful hears your words," said the Bondage-Breaker. "But why is your sister so quiet? Does she not realize what she has done? Every deed, good or bad, has an impact."

The whirlwind lifted off the ground. It became part of the large wind that swirled near the camp's edge. The three watched it go, then Brother turned toward his sister. Fear spread across his face.

"What is it?" she asked, as he backed away in horror.

"Your hand!"

A hope-shattering screech escaped her lips. Part scream, part moan, part whimper. Her legs collapsed under her and she buried her face in the sand. The rest of her body trembled, and she stretched her right hand out, as far from her heart as she could reach, as if it would contaminate the rest of her body.

The hand moments before had been healthy and graceful. It beautifully expressed the dances of Bondage-Breaker before the people. Now that hand was swollen and deformed, covered with open, oozing, inflamed sores. Her fingers were twisted and her knuckles bloody and the flesh drained of life. The skin was the deathly white of the snow.

Such a disease was one of the greatest terrors of the people. It meant a slow death and it was an abomination for the sufferer to be in the camp exposing others. Now she stood before the Special Place itself.

Brother turned to General. "Please, help her. Don't let her die."

General looked toward the watching wind. He called to Bondage-Breaker.

"You are the source of all beauty and health. Please return these to my sister's hand."

"Because of your faithfulness I will honor your request," said the wind. "I will return her hand to beauty and health. But she must go outside the camp for the seven days required. On the morning of the eighth day her hand will be normal and she may go through the ritual of cleansing and return."

The sister lifted her head and looked at General. "I don't deserve healing. I have been selfish."

"We are all selfish," said General. "But Bondage-Breaker is kind to us, so we should be kind to others."

They accompanied her to the edge of the camp. Sister walked alone toward the desert.

A cycle of the moon passed and then another. The People of the Promise followed the whirlwind northeast until it stopped on the edge of the new land.

"Why have we stopped?" asked the people.

"To see if you are ready," said the wind.

"Of course we are ready," proclaimed the people.

"We will see," said the whirlwind. It lifted from the ground and disappeared.

Suddenly the earth shook and lightning flashed across the sky. The people ran to their tents and hid.

As the storm calmed, families timidly peeked out. Showers fell in the distance and the sun sparkled through the rain. Colors arched over the new land and the people remembered the ancient promise:

"He is always close and he will always care."

EPILOGUE

The old man sat silent in the shadows of the dying embers with the night story still fresh on his tongue. The people knew it was over, but they didn't move. They watched the one with a hundred wrinkles and waited lest he say one more word. But the story was over.

Ten nights and ten stories. Each with its lesson and its challenge. Each shaping the people who listened with such hungry ears.

Slowly the people lifted themselves from the dry, sandy ground and drifted toward their tents. It was long past time for sleep.

A girl child ran to the ancient storyteller and took his callused hand. "I'm so glad they've arrived at the land," she blurted out.

"Oh granddaughter, to arrive does not mean to enter."

The nine-year-old child looked up in confusion.

"It is late," said the man with a chuckle as darkness swallowed the last light. "Tomorrow when we gather again you will understand."

The young one took the hand of the old one and asked, "Won't they walk the new land?"

"Bondage-Breaker will lead them to the highlands, but they must be willing to follow."

"I would," said the girl child.

"I know," said the storyteller. "To those who follow, Bondage-Breaker becomes Land-Giver."

The man lifted the sleepy child into his ancient arms and carried her toward her family tent. She slipped into dreams of walking with Bondage-Breaker through the hills of the new land.

Part 2
Land-Giver

TABLE OF CONTENTS
LAND-GIVER

PROLOGUE

Night had fallen quickly but the people were still impatient.

The circle waited and the fire blazed and a desert owl could be heard flying low seeking prey. The old man with the long, gray beard stepped to the center. His wool robe glowed as flames kept the cold and darkness at bay. He stroked his tangled beard thoughtfully as he surveyed the men and women and children. They were a small band of simple, hard-working shepherds who seemed to almost instinctively know how to glean truth from the harvest of history. They sat quietly in cross-legged fashion. They watched him as he watched them.

The one with a hundred wrinkles turned his face toward the ground and scooped up a handful of sandy soil. He held the dirt high above his head in his right fist and let it slowly filter through his wrinkled fingers. A soft evening breeze caught the sand and suspended each grain in the illumination of the firelight as, one by one, they fell again to the earth.

"There is always the land."

He spoke quietly. "As long as there is a Land-Giver there is a land for us. It may be conquered and taken away and abused. But always it belongs to Land-Giver and so do we.

"All else changes. But there is always the land," he said as he swept his hands to take in all of their surroundings. Then he held his hands out toward the stars. "And there is always Land-Giver."

The people were ready.

The time was right.

The man with a hundred wrinkles rubbed the remaining dirt from his fingers, and each listener leaned forward.

The story began.

TURNING POINTS COME QUICKLY. TO MISS THEM MEANS FAILURE, OR WORSE, IRRELEVANCY.

CHAPTER 1

THE SCOUTS

Don't be afraid!"

The voice of General carried through the camp.

"Step forward," said General. "Walk with me along the ridge of your new home. For Bondage-Breaker will now be Land-Giver to you and your children."

The people listened but there was a rumble of low voices.

And few moved toward the general.

Two elders approached. "The people have come to feel safe in this desert. The new land is unknown and uncertain and fearsome."

The other spoke low and earnestly: "Send scouts ahead. Let them explore the land and look at our road ahead."

"The road behind speaks loudly enough," said General sadly. "It reminds of plagues that did not destroy us and waters we crossed with dry feet. Our way has been strewn with drowned enemies and lit by fire. Do we who pick our bread from the desert sand need scouts?"

General spoke to all the people from the entrance to the Special Place. He selected twelve strong and hardy explorers. The leader of this small band was the commander who had led them to victory against the desert raiders. This young man drew courage from walks with Bondage-Breaker before the sun peaked above the Mountains of the Dawn. He often stood at General's side as a rock of stubborn faith. The people called him Point Man for he was always ready to lead in crisis.

On a hot and dry midsummer's morning General sent the twelve. "Study the land that will be our home. Follow Land-Giver and bring back the land's fruits."

"We will explore," agreed Point Man. "We will return with the fruits of our new home."

General watched until the twelve were specks climbing the distant ridge toward the hill country beyond his vision. For now it was out of sight. But soon he himself would walk the land. At last he would find peace and rest. The thought lifted his burdened heart.

Carefully, stealthily to avoid farmers and women washing clothes in streams, the scouts worked their way north. They took the hardest paths to the highlands between the Great Sea and the Salt Sea. These were least traveled. They continued north past the ruins of the City of Lime and past the Place of the Portal. They went on to the headwaters of the Winding River. Voices of ancestors beckoned onward into the land of promise.

They skillfully mapped rivers and valleys and hills. They noted farmlands and vineyards and orchard lands. Not until the twelve stood in the shadow of the snow-capped mountain in the far north did they turn back, reflecting on all they had seen. The land was rich and overflowing with grain and figs and almonds. It offered an abundance unknown in two years of desert wandering.

"The Land-Giver has led us to a good home," said Point Man.

"By this time next year we'll be snug in real houses. We'll be working our land," said his best friend, Companion.

But at this the remaining ten grew quiet and gazed uncomfortably into the dancing campfire flames. For the twelve had not journeyed alone. A snake had shadowed them. It had curled close as they slept—hissing fear into their ears:

"Has this land indeed been *given*? All around are high-walled cities with mighty armies and more weapons than you slaves in the wilderness have ever seen. What dreamers to think of marching into this fortress country! Will its residents just pack up and move? You can't take it from them."

Now the ten huddled together after Point Man and Companion were asleep. Now they voiced faithless words that had been whispered in their ears. Now they lay with a hand on their swords and imagined dangerous warriors creeping through the night shadows. The snake wandered away smugly. How easy it had been since that first encounter with Garden-Maker's faithless creatures. "You will lose, Land-Giver. Fear will swallow their faith and they will turn away," he snickered.

But he had not gained the ear of every spy. Point Man and his friend had not swerved from their confidence. He could find no stronghold in their hearts. So he ignored them. They slept soundly while the ten fled armies with bloody swords through restless dreamlands.

As they traveled south the spies studied the land's considerable defenses. They sketched watchtowers and thick city walls of tightly-fitting stone. Soldiers marched in and out of these cities. They were large soldiers with bronze and leather armor that made their muscles bulge all the more. They carried double-edged swords and spears and heavy battle-axes.

The ten trembled. The two wondered in awe what great deeds Land-Giver was about to accomplish.

A wind blew against their faces. "Don't forget who I am. Impossibilities have never stopped me from keeping my word."

One morning the twelve walked down a gentle slope into a section scented with honeysuckle and lilac.

Birds sang.

A doe drank from a still pond.

A frog splashed into the water.

"This is the most wondrous place we have seen," said Point Man. "We have reached the Valley of Apples, the home of our ancestors."

It seemed a paradise with apple and pomegranate and apricot trees. But the grapes drew special attention. Nowhere had they seen such large and deeply purpled globes.

"This must have been what the Garden was like," whispered Companion. The others nodded silently.

But soon they saw another wonder in this paradise valley—the shadow of the greatest of walled cities. Huge and powerful men stood guard with iron-tipped spears. The sun cast a glint off knives strapped to their sides.

"We wouldn't have a chance against even one of them," said a scout.

"We can't leave until we cut some fruit," said Point Man. "I promised General and we have seen none better."

"You made the promise so you keep it," said one of the faithless. "We are intruding on a great people in their valley."

"This is no longer their valley," responded Point Man. "We are standing in the midst of our home."

"Why don't you explain it to them?" said one. He pointed toward a column of soldiers approaching the city.

In the end the twelve bore away what fruit they could carry. Two left reluctantly; ten gratefully turned their faces toward the desert. They skirted the city and dropped into a smaller valley beyond the dark shadow. Here the grapes were even larger than the others they had seen. They selected their harvest by the light of a full moon that made the grapes glow on their twisted and weathered vines. They tied a sparkling cluster to a sturdy pole. The grapes on the vine weighed as much as a grown woman.

As they walked the banks of a stream carrying their grapes, they filled their bags with pomegranates and figs. The two named this beautiful place the Valley of Grapes. The ten cared not what it was called. They intended never to see it again.

Two million cheers went up as the twelve returned. General stepped forward with great ceremony.

"What have our twelve explorers found?"

Point Man unrolled large sheepskin maps. "The land is rich. There are deep rivers and high hills and fruit such as this. There also are large cities for Land-Giver to overcome. They are too great for us." Point Man indicated several places on the maps. "The cities are well fortified. Their walls stretch to the sky. In the Valley of Apples is the greatest of them. It has mighty warriors. Whatever way we enter the land, we must conquer it."

"So what should we do?" asked General.

"Go right up the middle and rejoice in what the Land-Giver has promised!" said Companion excitedly.

"You fool," said a spokesman for the ten. "Point Man has only begun to describe the greatness of these peoples. Grasshoppers might as well face giants."

"They do seem like giants and maybe we are grasshoppers," admitted Point Man. "But he who holds stars in his hands has promised us the land. If we enter with him it will be ours."

"If we enter the land we will all die," said a voice.

"The giants will laugh as they cut us down," said another.

"I place my trust in Land-Giver," shouted Point Man.

That night fear spread through the people like a sickness. The voices of the ten faithless had overpowered the words of Point Man and Companion.

"We can't go forward," said some. "We must return to the Land of Pyramids. If we humble ourselves before Delta King he will accept us back."

The next morning Point Man again stood before the people. "I know you are afraid. But don't turn your back on our new home and Land-Giver."

"Bondage-Breaker is no Land-Giver," screamed several in the crowd. "He says he cares but leaves us to rot in the desert."

"Don't be frightened," said General with Brother on one side and Point Man on the other. "You know Land-Giver. Who are giants to stand before him?"

"You lie," said one group of men as they picked up stones menacingly. "You will destroy us. We want a new general—one who will take us toward the setting sun."

Rapidly this was becoming a mob. Young men jumped onto the rock where the leaders stood and pushed them to the ground. Angry people encircled them clutching sharp rocks. They screamed and spit and kicked them with a viciousness that warmed the heart of Shining One.

"Land-Giver, help us! Open their eyes to who you are!"

Suddenly the whirlwind rose from the Most Hallowed Chamber and set down in front of the Special Place. It spun until it glowed fire and a voice roared from its center: "How long will these people disbelieve? When will they trust my words and follow my ways?"

Hundreds of stones dropped to the ground with a single thud. The mob backed away and hung their heads low.

"I will strike them here," boomed the glowing whirlwind. "They are not worthy to live in my land."

"Don't!" implored General. "You have been so patient, but stretch your mercy to cover even this. They still don't understand."

"I will have mercy for your sake," said the wind. "But they will die in their safe desert. Their children will till the rich new land and rest beneath its beautiful trees. Of this generation I will preserve only two—Point Man and Companion. For all the rest I now close the way."

The people stood still, caught between confusion and contemplation.

"Let's go back to the Land of Pyramids," shouted one of the ten faithless scouts. But before the sound of the sentence had stilled all ten choked and stumbled. A few staggered to their tents mumbling incoherently. Relatives and friends tried to cool their raging fevers. By night all ten faithless scouts were dead.

A chastened people mourned the judgment of Land-Giver. Most had now changed their minds about the land. None wanted to live out their lives in the desert.

"Land-Giver said he would give us the land so we should take it."

"If you had stepped forward when Land-Giver first spoke, the land would be yours," said General. "Now it belongs to the children."

"We have learned and we are ready. We will step forward and walk with Land-Giver along the ridge of our new home."

"Land-Giver has closed the way. He will not go with you. You will face your enemies alone."

Most listened but some who refused raised their own army and marched off to show Land-Giver their changed hearts. Only a few scattered fighters returned. They were beaten and bloody. When any of these warriors was asked later about the battle, they swallowed hard and mumbled: "To enter without Land-Giver is foolish."

NEGATIVITY FUELS DISCONTENTMENT; AN EFFECTIVE LEADER CONSTANTLY BATTLES BOTH.

CHAPTER 2

THE WANDERING

A great mass moved about a lonely landscape. Heat waves blurred the monotonously cloudless sky. Sweat rolled from furrowed brows. Tired and callused and sun-blistered feet marked the ancient caravan route. Merchant might have passed this way. Dreamer walked such a road bound for slave markets in the Land of Pyramids. But the blowing sand covered all traces of those who passed.

Little was said—dry mouths and cracked lips kept them quiet. Their journeys were dogged by a hopeless realization. They would travel until they were buried in these sands.

Little distinguished each passing year except marriages and births and burials. The daily concern was for water and food. When a suitable site was reached the people camped until their flocks stripped it of everything edible. Then they moved on in search of the next oasis. The desert was empty and unforgiving. Restless and weary, the people complained until the leaders reminded them of the care and kindness of Land-Giver.

But a few leaders fanned discontent. One such was a fat bald man with an eloquent tongue whose job it was to carry the Special Place's golden candelabra on their journeys. He was respected. Among those who listened and followed him were two defiant brothers filled with bitter anger. One evening as General and Brother sat before their fire a delegation of hundreds of esteemed men approached. Bald Man stepped forward.

"Why is yours the voice to tell us what to do and where to go?" he demanded.

"I only say what Land-Giver tells me," said General.

"You alone know what Land-Giver wants?"

General lowered his head and spoke softly but firmly, "Land-Giver chooses to whom he speaks. He chooses one who will listen and walk with him."

"It is not Land-Giver but you and your brother who have led us astray," said Bald Man. "You have taken us into the desert, away from the fertile land we were promised."

"Because the land is closed to us."

"A stronger leader would have persuaded us to step forward and claim the land."

"Perhaps," said General.

"It is time to choose a new guide."

The crowd cheered at this and the two defiant brothers sprang forward and bodily grabbed General and Brother—shoving them into the crowd. Some were stunned at this sudden move toward violence. Others wildly kicked and spit upon and cursed the aged men.

"Stop!"

General's command froze the crowd. Slowly he stood and helped Brother to his feet. "If you wish to contend with me for leadership, let us meet at the Special Place with the new day."

"Where is Bald Man? Where are the two defiant brothers?" asked General the next morning.

"In their tents with their wives and children," said one of the delegation with a guffaw. "They will come when they are ready."

"Don't they yet understand? It is not by my authority that we are gathering, but at the word of Land-Giver. He is patient but he will deal harshly with those who refuse to listen and harden their hearts and defy the one above all."

"What is your hurry?" yelled another. "If we follow you we are stuck out here for another twenty summers. What is an hour more or less?"

A great number outside the courtyard strained to see and hear. Some sided with General and some with the others, but most were shocked at the disrespect for General. He had led them so long. General turned away from the several hundred and marched through the multitude toward the tents of the bald man and the two defiant brothers. It took some time to reach them for they had set themselves apart from the rest of the camp.

"Move away from these tents," General commanded the crowd. "If Land-Giver chooses these men I will follow. But if he does not, let all remember that a hard heart leads to death."

The ground trembled and groaned. Onlookers pulled back in panic, and some were trampled in the confusion.

The earth cracked open.

The people gasped in horror.

The three tents were swallowed.

For just a moment there could be heard desperate screams in the chasm. Then the fissure closed and all was quiet. No sign was left that anything had stood there.

A shudder ran through the crowd, then all ran for their tents in terror.

"Assemble the followers of Bald Man," General told the elders. A far more reluctant group now gathered before the Special Place. No one stayed away.

"Bald Man showed himself unfit to lead," called General. "Which of you is ready? Whom do you wish Land-Giver to choose to take this people across the wilderness? Who among you listens for the voice of Land-Giver?"

There was silence.

"Who among you rises before the sun and walks with Land-Giver?"

Again silence.

"Which of you has given your newborn sons the cut of commitment?"

The silence was heavy and oppressing

"Then why would Land-Giver find you fit to lead his people?"

"But you have failed us!" shouted one brave soul.

"Why should we follow you?" shouted another.

"You've led us out to die one by one in this awful place!" cried a third.

Their confidence somewhat bolstered, all the several hundred agreed.

"So be it. Let Land-Giver make his choice," said General.

The Special Place rumbled and quaked. The whirlwind rose above the Most Hallowed Chamber and spun furiously. It spun faster until the wind itself seemed to catch fire above their heads. No one dared look at the intense light but all felt the explosion of heat and flame as a burst of white-hot light struck the ground. Then all was suddenly still.

Several hundred small piles of ash marked where the delegation had once stood. A hot breeze rustled through the camp until even the ashes were dispersed into the desert. It would have seemed as if none of them had existed were it not for the rising wails of their wives and children.

General also buried his head on Brother's shoulder and sobbed. "It is so simple," he gasped. "All we must do is follow. How many more will die before they understand?"

"They look for easier ways to get what they want," said Brother.

"But what do they want?"

"Anything lying just outside their grasp."

"But Land-Giver is what they need and he is so close," sighed General in exhaustion. "Even now they can have what will make them happy. It is so easy."

"Shining One confuses them. He whispers dark desires and delightful dreams into their ears."

"So now their false leaders are dead. Will they listen to Land-Giver?"

"Shining One's whispers are very sweet."

By the next morning Brother's words about Shining One were already coming true. The camp was astir as complaints arose from restless tongues.

"General has killed our leaders."

"His brother is conspiring with him against us."

"They will kill us all."

"General and Brother are unfair and vindictive and unfit to lead," it was said. Again a mob formed, feeling safety in the mass of their friends. The people picked up stones and moved as one toward the Special Place where General and Brother were sacrificing a spotless newborn lamb to Land-Giver.

"How many lessons must I require before the people are satisfied and trust in my care?" asked the whirlwind.

The people encircled the Special Place and shouted for the two. When General and Brother finished their sacrifice they faced the mob. Those closest raised their rocks and took aim, but once more the whirlwind rose. A voice called to General and Brother: "Move away from the people. Now I will end this defiance."

General and Brother moved away. Rock throwers moved to intercept them. But before the stones left their hands,

they turned pale

and their knees buckled

and they lay gasping for breath.

Their bodies shook and went still. Five fell then fifty then a hundred.

Death moved across the crowd. Five hundred fell then a thousand then five thousand.

General turned to Brother: "Take incense and fire from the golden altar. Run to stand between the living and the dead and cry for mercy to Land-Giver."

The brother ran for the altar. In a minute he stood on the line between the living and the dead. He held a bowl of fire in one hand and a bowl of incense in the other. Quickly he sent a cloud of incense into the spinning whirlwind. "Please spare your people. We don't deserve mercy but give us another chance to listen to you who holds stars in his hands."

Those to Brother's right remained healthy and well. Not one lived on his left. The people stared at the corpses then at Brother who had stood between them and the dead. They mourned the fallen, for each family had lost someone and whole tents now stood empty. But the people were thankful for life and they knew that only Brother, their keeper of the Special Place, had saved them.

"It was not I but Land-Giver who placed his hand across the crowd and kept death from taking more," Brother responded.

The people stood before the Special Place and asked Land-Giver to forgive their rebellion. Then they went into the desert and buried nearly fifteen thousand bodies—individuals whose hearts had been no harder than their own. Each realized he had done nothing to deserve life. And they began to understand why the spotless lambs were sacrificed and why it was so important to listen to Land-Giver.

Time passed and the people listened to Land-Giver and followed General and Brother. Brother taught his two sons and his sons' sons and even *their* sons the responsibilities of standing before Land-Giver. He gave each new generation in his family the cut of commitment and instructed them carefully.

Since the people had seen incense hold back death, most now understood that being keeper of the Special Place was no light matter.

The vital importance of this office stirred the next dissension. Some questioned whether Land-Giver had really given this privilege only to one family. But no one spoke of this until General called together the leaders of each of the twelve ancestral tribes.

"Land-Giver has heard your whispers and will confirm those who will keep the Special Place. Each leader should bring a shepherd's staff marked with the tribal sign."

"How will he let us know so there will be no doubt as to whom he has chosen?" asked one of the leaders.

"I will place the twelve staffs in the Most Hallowed Chamber where Land-Giver dwells. These staffs will lie before the ark of mystery. Land-Giver will touch one and life will flow into it. That tribe will be known as keepers of the Special Place forever."

Early the next morning General reverently pulled back the curtain and stood before the ark of mystery. The golden ark glowed and in the shadows he could see that one staff had been touched with life. He carried them into the courtyard and set each in front of its owner. The final staff was placed before Brother and all stared in amazement. His staff had grown buds and branches. Pink flowers blossomed beside green leaves. Hidden in the foliage were sweet almonds.

None doubted that Brother's tribe was chosen but now amazement turned to terror.

"Will the ground swallow us with our families?"

"Will flames turn us to ash?"

"Will we fall dead?"

"We have been foolish," said one of the leaders. "We will respect and honor the position of Brother as well as the leadership of General."

His words became a pledge that was made throughout the camp.

The People of the Promise brought spotless newborn lambs to the copper altar in the courtyard of the Special Place.

"I think the people now understand," said General to Brother.

A sweet smoke rose above the camp.

Land-Giver smiled in delight.

CHAPTER 3

THE FINAL YEAR

The night of nights was the distant memory of only a few. Thirty-nine years had faded since the angel of death passed over the People of the Promise and entered the houses of the pyramid. Thirty-seven years had faded since General stood at the edge of the new land. Here he stood again looking north with Brother on one side and his sister on the other. Over a hundred summers had passed since a baby was set adrift in a basket. Now that baby was aged and stood with his older brother and sister.

"A year from now we shall enter the new land," General said.

"I am not certain of that," said Brother.

"But Land-Giver said that after the passing of a generation we could return to this spot and the way would be open."

"Land-Giver said that of our generation he would preserve only two—Point Man and Companion. He said that when all had died the next generation could return. Then the way would be open."

"Surely Land-Giver will not keep us out. It has been so long. We have served him so hard," mused General.

"We are the last of the generation," Sister reminded gently.

"We are the oldest in the camp.

"We are the ones who must pass leadership to our children."

"But our bodies are still strong and our minds are still quick," insisted General.

"Not so strong as when we crossed the sea," said Brother. "Not so quick as when we last prepared to enter the land."

"I fear you are right," said General as he looked wistfully northward, "but I long to walk the new land. I long to see the Valley of Apples and the Valley of Grapes."

"But the best road is with Land-Giver, even if it is beyond the sky."

"Especially if it is beyond the sky," added Sister.

General nodded but his hope was still strong. Oh, if he could take this final step with the people.

"Please come!" said the young boy who breathlessly stumbled into General's tent. "What is it, great-grandson?" General asked as he jerked awake.

"It is Sister! She needs you."

The Brother knelt beside the pallet of blankets, his face barely visible in the pale glow of the hanging lamp. The woman whose hand he grasped seemed pale and lifeless. A grimace of pain crossed her face.

"What is wrong?"

"I will not stand in the Valley of Apples with you," she whispered. "Land-Giver is giving me a better land and he is calling now."

"But we are not ready to let you go," said General.

"You are not strong enough to stop me," said his sister. "My days have been full. What an adventure we have had. But it is time to part for just a little while."

"Please don't leave us." Brother's voice cracked.

One last squeeze of his hand.

"Soon. We will meet. . . . Very. . . ."

A smile crossed her lips as she looked at last upon Land-Giver and stepped to his side. Together they walked toward marvelous places beyond the sky. Not seeing all of this the two brothers wept. The news spread through the camp. For a full cycle of the moon the camp mourned. Preparations stopped. Everyone knew Sister, so the outpouring of emotion was great. It was greater than any death the people could remember. But there was something more. Each man and woman felt they were nearing the end— and were at the beginning—of wondrous things. It was so hard. It was so sad. It was so. . .yes, it was so exciting!

During the mourning period all supplies of water were drawn dry. The sun blazed hot and the people's throats grew parched. The livestock suffered while the oldest and the youngest died of thirst. The people forgot their excitement and began complaining once more. Once again their quarrels were directed toward General and Brother.

"We are in the final year of our wandering," said the people. "And now we will die of thirst. We stand on the edge of our new home and all ve need is water to keep our hopes alive but where is it?"

"Look to Land-Giver for your hopes, not water!" shouted General, itter that such grumbling invaded his grief. "If we need water, he can peak and a river will flow through the driest of deserts."

"Sister is gone," cried the people. "Perhaps Land-Giver is also leaving us."

"Have you forgotten the promise of the rainbow?" asked General. He is always close and he will always care."

"We have not seen a rainbow for years," one angry elder reminded him.

"Leave me! I will see to your water," grumbled General. His heavy heart was filled with anger and self-pity and sorrow. He turned from the people and faced the Special Place.

The whirlwind rose before him. Its power and presence bent his knees. It sparkled and glowed with such intensity that General hid his face.

"Gather the people," said the wind. "Go to the outcropping of rock vest of camp. Speak to the rock: 'From the hardest rock pours the unlimited love of Land-Giver!' Then step back, for I will show that I will meet heir every need."

The great flat space near the rock was soon filled with hopeful yet doubtful people. *Almost all of the people I have known and loved have fallen n the desert,* thought General. And now a new multitude had been raised up to replace them. If only they would have more faith than their parents. such great things could happen.

But a great many were not believing.

"There's no water out here!" yelled one man near the front. Hundreds eem to nod their heads in agreement.

"The ground is so hard and dry. Nothing can live in this terrible place!" yelled another.

'Be quiet!" shouted General. "My brother and I are sick of your complaints." He held his shepherd's staff high and said, "This is the staff empowered by Land-Giver.

"It has become a snake

"and separated a sea

"and won a war.

"And still you do not believe."

"All we know are stories of things that happened many years ago!" elled a woman. Many people added their voices to agree.

"All right!" shouted General. His face flamed. "Once more I will giv
you water!"

"Prove it!" demanded the people.

The staff struck the rock with a loud crack. Then it came dow
again—harder and louder. The ground shook. The rock shuddered an
rumbled and vibrated. A piece of jagged rock quivered then was pushe
from the stone face by the force of water. The sound of rushing wate
reached everyone's ears. Suddenly it burst into an enormous geyser, shoot
ing higher and higher into the sky.

Water rained down upon those nearby. They opened their mouth
wide and looked skyward. The water splashed their dusty faces and trick
led down their parched throats. Children danced and laughed and played
The fountain drenched all who stepped forward. Someone shouted an
pointed skyward. A hush fell over the people.

The late afternoon sun reflected off the most beautiful rainbow.

A young woman began singing, "He is always close and he will alway
care." The song spread until a thunderous crowd lifted the notes to heaven.

General smiled but a gnawing feeling ate at his heart.

Now the wind whistled in his ear.

"Did you do well?" asked Land-Giver. "Did you follow my words?"

"You know I did not," he said. His head hung low in humility. H
knelt on the wet rock. "I was so tired of their demands. I was angry tha
they did not believe you."

"You were angry that they did not believe *you,* not me," said th
wind. "You wanted to show your own power—more than you wanted t
show mine."

"You speak the truth. I have taken my eyes from you. I have stoler
your glory."

"You did not follow my way but your own. It is time you took m
path beyond the sky. You will not cross into the new land."

General's heart fell and he buried his face in his hands. Then slowly
he raised from his knees.

"All you say is right and fair.

"I must pay the price for my pride.

"Walk with me that I might wander no more."

"I always walk paths you can follow. Reach out. I will take your hand."
A cycle of the moon passed, then two, then three. Word came that a larg

and powerful army gathered to the east. The people moved south to avoid conflict and stopped in the shadow of a lofty mountain surrounded by a strange broken landscape of caves and canyons.

During the journey Brother's breath grew short. He stumbled frequently then fell face-down in the sand. Two strong men laid him carefully in a shaded wagon for those too ill to travel. A woman bathed his face. He drifted through a restless, fevered sleep.

Beside the lofty mountain General bent close. "By another sunset your sorrows will pass. You will join our sister and I will soon follow. Our long journey is almost over. Our rest land is won."

Brother revived in the cool of the morning, and his two humble sons lifted him onto a rough stretcher. With General and many strong young men, they started up the slope of the lofty mountain. General walked beside Brother and kept the sun's heat from his face. Together they spoke of their lives of adventure. They found a path through the rough terrain on which they could carry the stretcher. High on the mountain they finally set down the bed at a place where Brother could see faraway.

As the sun rested, the sons helped their father remove his coat. This was the coat of his office. It showed his place at the head of his tribe. It marked him as chief among the keepers. All watched in respectful silence as Brother folded it with trembling hands and passed it to his oldest living son. "Do the work of Land-Giver and the people. Never forget that you stand with the one above all. Once. . .I forgot. But he will forgive those who forget. He forgave. . . ."

The oldest son gently took the folded coat from his father.

"I will not forget. Land-Giver and I will stand together."

The sun was almost below the horizon when Brother blessed his two humble sons. Then he turned to General.

"Soon. . .very soon. . .we will meet."

"It will be a meeting of joy."

The world shifted into shadows and darkness settled on Brother. One last cough and a final sigh and Brother rose from his bed to walk the edges of eternity with the wind.

General and Brother's sons could only imagine what it was like as they stood around the empty body and let the darkness engulf them.

A cool breeze dried away General's tears. In the darkness all was silent save the hushed sobs of his two nephews and the other young men.

"This is our final year," said General. "In seven cycles of the moon you shall enter the new land. I shall join my brother and sister beyond the sky."

"But who shall lead us?" asked Brother's eldest son. The weight of office already was heavy.

"Land-Giver will lead, as he has always led. And someone will be chosen to take my place before him. You are on an exciting threshold. I wish I could cross with you. But Land-Giver will soon take me. He has prepared another to stand before his people."

General looked up. Stars were breaking through the blackness—so bright and near they seemed ready to descend, ready to join the march into the new land.

"The one who holds those in his hand," General said as he pointed up, "will also hold you close. All you need to do is rise with the dawn and walk with him."

THE SCRAMBLE FOR RICHES
CREATES COMPROMISE
THAT RUSTS THE HEART,
TARNISHES THE REPUTATION,
AND PLUNDERS THE FUTURE.

CHAPTER 4

THE SORCERER

From the Plains of Comfort they would begin. The army would be mustered. The people would move out. The plains were named for the balsam trees that soothed and healed. Palms shaded and bestowed fruit. Here just north of the Salty Sea was a foretaste of the good land west of the Winding River.

The journey from the Lofty Mountain had not been easy. General ached for Brother and Sister. He longed to join them, even more than he longed to walk the new land. Point Man took the lead and faced three attacking armies. Three times Land-Giver gave complete victory. Finally they could rest, but half a day's walk toward the setting sun stood the mighty Fortress City. Its massive double walls stretched to the sky.

The Plains King watched the camp from a distance. The ragtag soldiers hardly deserved the name of an army. Yet he had seen these soldiers crush an enemy.

They were becoming disciplined.

They fought valiantly with the weapons at hand.

Some power made them seem unstoppable.

The king was worried. He stood between them and the land beyond the Winding River that they were ready to conquer. He stood and trembled.

"We must stop them," he told his advisors, "or our bodies will lie on fields of blood."

"But their numbers are so great," said a commander. "It will be difficult to crush them."

"We need something more than battle. We need help from one who can call forth powers from beyond."

That was the answer. It would only require a dark curse.

Messengers raced from the Plains King to the South Lands King. They must find the greatest sorcerer in the land. They must gather a treasure of silver and gold to buy his strongest magic. Twenty days north on the trade road between the City of Crossroads and the City of Caravans lived a famous sorcerer. He was powerful in the ways of Shining One. His curses were said to have brought destruction on armies. He was the one the kings would hire.

The sorcerer could not believe his good fortune: A delegation offered him greater riches than he knew existed. Of course he would call down death upon enemies of the great kings. Why, his curses might obliterate the enemy army even before it lined up for battle. Land-Giver laughed at the pretentious little man.

He rose early and saddled his donkey and turned south. His donkey trotted, for when the master was in a hurry he used his whip hard and frequently. This day he was in a great rush. Perhaps at least the donkey would find sweet water and tender stalks and some salt to lick. Maybe he would have the chance to give his rider a good kick.

Suddenly it seemed that a bag had been lifted from his head. He had seen with donkey eyes and heard with donkey ears and thought donkey thoughts. Now he saw and heard and thought things no donkey had seen or heard or thought before.

Standing in the way he saw a great figure of light. His shoulders were muscular and his face firm. He wore bright silver armor that glowed in the midday sun.

The donkey saw and heard the swish of a sword of flame.

The donkey thought it would be good to be faraway.

"Halt!" called the menacing figure. "You may not pass!"

The donkey stopped so quickly that Sorcerer nearly catapulted over his ears. The sorcerer saw and heard nothing. Shining One had long numbed his mind and shut his eyes to realities. He was determined to move ahead. Sharp blows landed on the donkey, so he turned off the road into a field.

The beating increased, accompanied by angry threats as the sorcerer tried to get his animal back on the road. Reluctantly the donkey returned to the road. But farther along where the road went between two walls, the glowing angel stood again with his silver armor and flaming sword.

The donkey slowed and pressed close to the wall in hopes of avoiding the swing of the angel's sword. But with this move, the sorcerer's foot was scraped painfully against the wall.

Again the whip.

The angel disappeared and the donkey made a run for it, and he bounced his passenger unmercifully. But ahead was an even more narrow gap. There the glowing being again appeared.

This utterly unnerved the beast. He dug in his heels and sat back on his haunches with a thud. The rider was dumped onto the ground without the modesty due a great sorcerer.

The sorcerer screamed and beat at the donkey. This was becoming intolerable. The donkey might have bolted if Land-Giver had not worked a wonder.

As far as the donkey knew, he brayed as loud a protest as he knew how. Only it came out in undonkeylike sounds:

"What have I done to you? Why have you beaten me these three times?"

The sorcerer stopped and stepped back and swung about. He almost tripped but no one was there. He turned back to his animal.

"What has gotten into you? You crushed my foot! You refuse to go!"

"But haven't I always been an obedient animal?" answered the donkey.

This time there was no mistaking the source. The shocked sorcerer sank back onto a rock. He stared at the donkey and the donkey stared back at him. The man nodded dumbly.

"Yes! So if I am now disobedient don't you think there must be a good reason?"

Heat, the sorcerer thought; *it's addled the brain.*

But he nodded again.

A light brighter than the sun unveiled itself in the road ahead. He rubbed his eyes. Land-Giver lifted his confusion and let him see the massive angel in silver armor clutching a sword of fire. He fell to the ground and hid his face.

"I have come to stop you," announced the angel. "Land-Giver will let none curse his people."

"But I don't. . . . I didn't know. . . . They are his people," stammered the sorcerer. "If I'd known I would never. . . . I will head on back and. . ."

"Silence! You will go to the kings. But you will carry the words of him who holds the stars in his hands, rather than a curse."

The sorcerer decided he might have trouble earning that silver and gold.

The Plains King took the sorcerer to a hilltop.

"There they are. Curse your most powerful curse."

"First, you must build seven altars and make a sacrifice on each one."

While the king arranged this, the sorcerer spoke to Land-Giver. "Accept my seven sacrifices. Please let me curse that people."

The sorcerer went back to the king—determined. He looked down on the camp, stood tall and opened his mouth to release a curse.

Instead words of blessing flowed.

"What are you doing?" demanded the king. "That is no help!"

"Land-Giver has turned my tongue from curse to blessing."

The king recovered his dignity. "All right. We will go higher. With a better perspective, you will have the advantage.

From the mountaintop they looked down on the camp. While the king built seven more altars and made sacrifices, the sorcerer spoke to Land-Giver: "Fourteen altars. Fourteen sacrifices. Surely now you will let me curse the people."

The sorcerer did his best. He stood tall and opened his mouth. But again his evil words did not come out. A second blessing flowed.

"You've done it again!" yelled the king. "If you do not curse these people, you will get no gold and I will send word to every kingdom that you are a fraud."

The king took the sorcerer to a third place. Once more the king built seven altars and made sacrifices. "This is my last chance," he told Land-Giver. Twenty-one altars and twenty-one sacrifices. I beg you: Be kind to me."

This time his words of blessing were stronger and sweeter than before. The sorcerer tried to stop, but the words tumbled out. The king burned and still the blessing flowed. The sorcerer spoke his final words:

". . . May those who bless these people be blessed and those who curse these people be cursed."

"I should kill you!" The king pounded his fist into his other hand. "You blessed *them* and cursed *us*."

The sorcerer sadly mounted his donkey for the long trek home. He was angry at the king for not paying and angry at himself for not cursing and angry at Land-Giver. He was most angry at Shining One for being powerless.

North of the Plains of Comfort the sorcerer's donkey once again stopped. "Not another angel," spat the sorcerer.

"I was once an angel," hissed the snake coiled in the middle of the road, "the fairest of angels."

"I know well who you are. You failed me."

"My power is of a subtle kind," said the snake with a half-smile. "Land-Giver thinks he is infinite and eternal and all-powerful," said the snake. "But if one is clever, there are ways around him."

"Tell me," begged the sorcerer.

"Tasty meats and sparkling wine and beautiful women will lead them to worship all manner of things. It doesn't matter what they worship. If it isn't Land-Giver, it is I," hissed the snake. He slithered from the road and disappeared between two rocks.

The sorcerer turned south. What he knew was worth many chests of gold.

Weeks later the Plains King and the South Lands King held an incredible festival to honor Shining One. Women in inviting clothing quietly appeared in the camp of the People of the Promise. "Come to the festival," they said. "Let us put aside fighting and enjoy one another. We can live in peace."

It sounded reasonable, especially from these messengers.

The festival was exciting and carefree—with real wine and more food than ever could be found in camp! There were laughter and dancing and subtle suggestions. As the night progressed, the dancing became more enticing and the wine stronger and the women more beautiful.

Land-Giver was forgotten.

Shining One was glorified.

All that is good and right and moral was abandoned.

The People of the Promise who went to the party did what they had never done before. The next morning they were sick and humiliated and guilt-ridden. Land-Giver was angry and sad.

"We are in great danger," General told the leaders. "Many have disobeyed and gone to the festival. Anarchy has entered the camp and anarchy leads to death. From this day every man and woman who follows Shining One must die. Each is a traitor against Land-Giver."

Mourning spread through the camp. The condemned wailed with their families. Those who killed them grieved as well. It was a dark moment for the young nation. Again General summoned Point Man and the leaders.

"We cannot live near the followers of Shining One. If we do, we will be destroyed. Land-Giver will destroy everything as he did before and his promises will be ruined. If we feel pity, we must put it aside. We must destroy so that we can save. Turn your warriors against the people of the south, for their king is still plotting our destruction."

Point Man led out twelve thousand warriors. There were a thousand from each tribe. They overwhelmed the enemy and killed every soldier. Even the greedy sorcerer was killed as he tried to sneak toward his northern home. His donkey could not take him away fast enough, for he was weighed down with gold and silver.

The People of the Promise burned the cities and castles they captured. The soldiers returned to rest beneath the palms and rubbed balsam oil on their wounds. Point Man reported to General.

"It is a hard thing you have done but Land-Giver is good," said General.

The whirlwind rose high above the Special Place and glowed a soft yellow. The people felt joy in their sorrow. They had pleased the one who holds the stars in his hands.

CHAPTER 5

THE PASSING AWAY

Y ou shall not cross the river," said the wind.

General sat on the bank of the Winding River and looked across to the new land.

"Your answer is unchangeable?"

"My answers never change," whispered the wind.

"To step onto that river bank would fulfill my dream."

"The feet of others will fulfill your dream."

General nodded in sad acceptance. "But it was a worthy dream."

"It was worthy but you are not," reminded the wind.

"Does one failure cast down my times of faithfulness?"

"Your faithfulness will bring a great nation across the Winding River. Your failure will keep only one from touching that soil. My discipline seems hard but it isn't rejection. It is almost time for your journey to my house."

"I am ready."

"First you must prepare the people," whispered the wind. "They must drive out the dwellers of the new land. You have seen just a little of the damage of mingling and marrying. Shining One will seduce them into anarchy. Gather the people and tell them all of my words."

It was the first day of the eleventh month of the final year. General stood on the highest hill near the camp. People sat and stood before him for as far as his eyes could see. So many had died. But so many had been born.

"How was it possible to sustain all of these in the desert?" General wondered aloud.

"Only Land-Giver could do such a work," said Point Man in awe. "And you were his willing tool in this wonder."

"Now, my son, you will be that tool."

The two million sat before their leader. He had aged much in the months since his brother's death. He looked out at the people, so eager for truth and leadership, as they watched his every move. He looked beyond them to the river he would never cross and the land his feet would never touch. Those close saw that tears blurred his vision and sadness filled his voice. Heralds stood in their places to shout the words on back to the farthest people.

Most understood that this was their leader's last message.

"Enter the land, my people, but above all else seek him who gives it to you. He alone gives the land meaning:

"He lives beyond the sky but dwells among you.

"He holds stars in his hands but stooped to plant the garden.

"Nations are too small to hold him but a single heart is big enough.

"He is Promise-Keeper and Bondage-Breaker and Land-Giver. You will know him by yet other names if you listen to his words and follow his ways. He is always close and he will always care."

The people cheered and promised that they would never forget.

General spoke through the day's heat. Mothers listened while tending their infants. The oldest held tightly to the words of one who was far older.

"Long ago on the mountain, Land-Giver gave us ten powerful words to make our lives good. He told us to:

"Listen and reflect on them.

"Memorize and follow them.

"And never let our children forget them.

"He told us to teach the words to our children and our children's children."

All the people agreed that they would reflect and follow and teach.

"Are you truly willing to take the words into the New Land and to obey them with all your heart and all your soul?"

One by one and ten thousand by ten thousand, a sea of people rose to their feet. Two million men and women and children stood in the blazing heat of the Plains of Comfort. Tears streamed down the face of General as he saw the people's commitment.

"Soon you will cross the river and conquer the New Land. When you are there, find a high place where all can see, and build a monument of uncut stones. Build it tall, of white stone, so it will stand like sparkling snow against the blue sky. Then when you look upon it and when you show it to your children and their children, remember the commitment you made on the Plains of Comfort."

General lifted his shepherd's staff above his head. "Whoever holds this staff will lead you across the river. That person must be strong and courageous. He must not be afraid nor easily discouraged."

Without another word General walked to where Point Man stood with the elders. He handed him the staff and the two embraced. Two million cheers went up. The noise could be heard in the Fortress City across the river.

General called for his two nephews—the keepers of the Special Place. Young men brought great rolls of beautifully preserved skins. The skins were covered with writing. These rolls were passed to the keepers of the Special Place.

"These are the journals of our people. They tell of the making of the garden and of the forming of our father and mother. They tell of the coming of Shining One. They tell of Merchant and the promises made by Promise-Keeper. They tell how Bondage-Breaker brought you from the Land of Pyramids and gave you his ten words and how to serve and obey him.

"Guard my journals—for they are not my words alone. They are the deeds and words of the one who holds the stars. He has given them to his people. You and Point Man will add to them the great works Land-Giver will do and the great words he will say."

General sang a song. His voice was strong. His words floated through the great throng until all took up the words and melody.

He is our rock;
We are his people.
Let us never be foolish;
Let us never forget.
Yes, he is our refuge
And we are his children.

When his last phrase was passed along by the farthest heralds, the sun was descending to the horizon. One of the elders came and spoke his heart.

"You have been a great leader," he told General. "Forgive us for turning against you and failing to give support to your hands."

General held out his hands to bless the people. He was exhausted and drawn from the exertion of the day. Then he and Point Man turned from the great multitude and its tears. Alone they walked toward the mountain.

Together they spoke of the past and the future and the keeper of both.

"Be strong and courageous," said General in a parting benediction.

Then he alone climbed on. Point Man watched the stooped, solitary figure fade into the night shadows. Wispy clouds clung to the mountaintop and Point Man watched until his hero had disappeared. Then he turned to walk slowly back toward the camp. The work had passed to him, and he felt quite lonely.

A brilliant flash illuminated the mountaintop for the twinkling of an eye. In that flashing moment Point Man thought he saw a glowing angel with sparkling white robe and large shiny wings descend to embrace the solitary man who had seen the silhouette of the one above all.

For a cycle of the moon, the people mourned. Point Man climbed the mountain to find and lay the body to rest. But there was no trace of General. He stood on the highest plateau where the sorcerer had stood to curse the people. Spread before him was the camp of the People of the Promise.

"What are you looking for?"

The voice startled Point Man from his reverie. He stood to face a being whose very arms and face glowed like the sun. Point Man fell to his knees and looked to the ground to shield his eyes.

"I seek General," answered Point Man.

"His spirit is beyond the sky."

"His body?"

"Land-Giver sent me to bury it," said the angel. "It lies hidden deep within the earth."

"Is there a place where we can honor his memory?"

"It is an unmarked grave in a nearby valley."

"So how shall we honor this great man?"

"Honor him throughout the new land.

"Honor him by keeping the words of Land-Giver.

"Honor him by following the one who holds the stars in his hands."

Point Man smiled in understanding. Suddenly the angel was gone, but the wind blew strong. General's words seemed to echo on it as it whistled through the mountain rocks:

"Be strong and courageous.

"Be strong and courageous.

"Be strong and courageous."

CHAPTER 6

THE INN-KEEPER

In three days we will cross the river. The conquering time has begun. Soon the New Land will belong to us."

Leading elders of the families had anticipated Point Man's words but they were charged with the thrill and fear of the moment. They looked beyond the sky and stamped their staffs in agreement.

"Tell your soldiers to sharpen their swords.

"Tell the people to pack their belongings and gather their livestock.

"Tell all to fast and give homage to him who gives us the land."

One stepped forward and embraced Point Man's shoulders. "Be strong and courageous. We will do what you say and follow where you lead. As General commanded us, so now we give our lives into your hand."

"Follow me as far as I follow the one who is infinite and eternal and all powerful," answered Point Man.

Point Man had prepared for this day. He had set watchers in the hills. Spies gathered information about the surrounding armies. He had found travelers willing to teach the languages of the peoples ahead. Now he called for two of his best watchers.

"You well know how closely our enemies have shadowed us," said Point Man. "They looked on at the three battles before we reached the Plains of Comfort. They saw and feared and then sent the young daughters of Shining One to dance with our young men. They watched us mourn General."

"Why haven't they attacked?" asked one of the watchers.

"I only know that Land-Giver is our shield. I need eyes and ears to know more. "

"Are we to be your eyes and ears?" asked one of the young soldiers with a confident grin.

"Scout the central highlands. Dress as travelers. Go north and cross the river. Take the road south to the Fortress City."

In old clothes they hid their youth. The watchers journeyed north and crossed the river and met a merchant caravan.

"We are wanderers whose sandals never stop and who seek our food through our hands."

"By your speech you have come a long distance for your food. Do you have skills?" asked the weathered old captain of the caravan.

"We have learned to do whatever is needed to fill an empty belly."

"We will soon reach the Fortress City and then go on to the Land of Pyramids. Strong backs and ready swords against desert raiders will be welcome."

"We have planned only so far as the Fortress City," said the lead watcher.

As they came over a rise, the merchants saw the sun's gleam on the distant city walls.

On the following day the two blended with travelers entering the northern gate. Each passed under the gaze of soldiers. Occasionally one was pulled roughly aside and questioned. The city was nervous.

In the market they mingled with the buyers and sellers. They listened and studied every detail.

"They will soon close the gates to outsiders," said a toothless old woman to her companion.

"What they fear I don't understand," said a man selling young sheep. "Desert bandits may come, but this city cannot be taken."

"These bandits have done things none thought possible. There are enough of them to cover the land," said a well-dressed man.

"They follow a powerful being who destroyed the army of the Land of Pyramids," said a seller of oils. "All who have fought them have been cut down."

"But can't Shining One protect us?" asked the little son of the well-dressed man.

"There," said the sheep seller. "Listen to that boy; he knows. We have Shining One and plenty of food and high walls. That's all it takes."

"I hope so," said the well-dressed man. His voice was tinged with doubt.

The watchers stayed too long without buying. They noticed a soldier eyeing them and slowly walked away, losing him along a crowded narrow alleyway around an ornate temple dedicated to Shining One. Where shops and houses were built into the inner wall, the watchers ducked into a dark room that smelled of stale wine and sweat. Too late they saw that many who ate at the long rough-hewn tables were soldiers. The two sat along the wall beside a friendly man who looked like a fellow traveler. His slurred words showed he had been there some time.

Soldiers were alternately boisterous and quietly serious. Their heavy swords hung from thick leather belts. Much was said in low voices as they emptied their wooden cups, but the watchers had keen ears.

"Starting tonight we watch double-close," said the commander.

"I hear there are more warriors coming than we have people in ten cities—all battle hardened," said a young soldier.

"That's close enough to the truth," said the commander.

"Maybe they will continue north."

"Our spies say they plan to conquer all the land. They believe it has already been given to them and all they need do is to claim it."

"Then our swords will show them a good battle."

"Don't be a fool. We won't fight them. We will bar the gates and sit tight while they tire themselves out banging on our doors. No desert army can take this city."

"Keep alert," said the commander. "Strangers were seen in the market. There probably are spies about. And here's one of them. . . . "

He playfully grabbed the waist of a tall, dark-skinned beauty who struggled to keep her bowls and cups balanced. She laughed and sent a knee into the ribs of the commander without spilling a drop. She set down the bowls and the soldiers plunged their hands into the food.

"Food or drink?"

She looked down at the two handsome strangers and coyly pushed back her long black locks as she waited to see their money.

"They seem to like both," said the oldest, pointing at the soldiers.

"They eat anything, but my food is best in the city," said the woman with a wink.

She had a self-assured air as she wandered from table to table, taking orders and keeping control. She was no slave.

Golden hoops hung from her ears.

Rings sparkled from her fingers.

An expensive silk was wrapped around her waist.

She held every eye, dressed with the garish attractiveness of one who sold more than food to her customers.

"Getting out of this city may be difficult," mumbled the younger spy.

"Let us eat and find a sleeping place. When the sun rises above the mountains we will mingle with other travelers at the southern gate."

"Why not now? The gates have not yet closed."

"That would be expected. We would not be seen beyond the city gates alive."

"Here's your food," the server interrupted with a smile. "It will satisfy your hunger." She set bread and meat and red wine before them. "And I would avoid talking," she added in a whisper. "People with strange accents are none too safe."

"Please," said the oldest quietly. "Do you have somewhere for two weary travelers to rest?"

"Perhaps," she said with a glance at the soldiers. "Later."

The watchers looked at one another. This must be someone they could trust. They had little choice. Silently the two watched the mangy dog that slept nearby wake periodically to snap up scraps.

The soldiers left and the inn quieted. The woman drifted to where they sat and slid softly next to the oldest, slipping her arm around him. But her eyes were cautious, not flirtatious.

"The two of you are near the end of your lives."

"The soldiers are gone."

"The man who sat by you is never so drunk as he seems. Some of my customers have lost their lives because they confided a secret near him. He is even now finding someone to sell you to," she said matter-of-factly.

"Where can we hide?"

"If I hide you, my life will be as short as yours."

"We serve Land-Giver. He will protect you," said the older. "We will be able to save your life later."

"Follow me," the Inn-Keeper said quietly.

She took the watchers to the high flat roof of the public house. It actually was built between the inner and outer walls. They could look out on the surrounding fields. They also could see soldiers moving about the streets, stopping passersby.

"No place is safe for you tonight," said the woman, "This is your best chance."

The roof was spread with piles of drying flax nearly ready to be beaten into pliable strands for weaving into coarse linen. The watchers lay near the side of the roof and were carefully covered to look like a pile of golden flax.

"If your Land-Giver will protect you, ask him to keep soldiers away from this section of the wall," said the woman. The sun's final rays of daylight were swallowed by shadow.

She was lighting the lamps hanging from the stucco ceiling when soldiers burst into the public house. Their eyes cast about the room. It was dim and nearly empty. They turned to the Inn-Keeper.

"You were busy today," said the commander.

"You all seemed to like my food and company," she said with a smile.

"Two strangers were here," said the commander.

"I serve many strangers. But I know the two you mean."

"We must find those two. They have not passed the gates."

She shrugged, and the covering slipped loosely and seductively from one of her shoulders. She did not push it back. "I passed a pleasant bit of time with them. They are gone."

"Where?" growled the commander. "You know more about what happens in this city than the king. Tell me what you heard or you will be a lovely offering in tomorrow's slave market."

"Why threaten? Why would I not tell you? I heard them say something about a way out of the city that did not pass through the gates. They seemed in a hurry."

"How did they learn about the passage?" the commander muttered. "Someone must have helped them."

"I would think so," the woman continued. "If it is a help, they mentioned the paths east toward the river."

"Why did you wait so long to give us this help?" the commander growled. In seconds the room was deserted.

"You can come out now," the Inn-Keeper said to the darkness of her roof. She could hear the rustle of flax as two heads poked cautiously from the bundles.

"They seek you at the river. They will search all night in one direction while you take another."

"You have saved our lives," said the leader. "What can we do for you?"

"Keep your promise," said the Inn-Keeper. "Spare me and my parents and brothers and sisters. I have heard much of Bondage-Breaker and Land-Giver from travelers. I know he is greater than Shining One. I know he will destroy this evil place. Many in this city are terrified of your greatness."

The Inn-Keeper took the watchers to a defense portal in the city wall above her inn. She threw down a long rope. "Go west to the caves in the hills. They will search for you three days. Then return to your people."

"Land-Giver will honor you," said the younger spy. "As soon as we gain the city, we will come for you and all who are in this room. All others in the city must die.

"When you see our armies, tie a strip of linen from this window, a strip that is long and scarlet."

The two slipped down the rope into the darkness. She searched out her longest bolt of brightest scarlet. Looking beyond the sky she begged, "Remember me. Help me leave my past. I want to follow you."

A warm wind blew through the window and a gentle voice whispered, "You will not be forgotten."

CHAPTER 7

THE VICTORY

Even the king sleeps in terror," reported the watchers to Point Man. "Land-Giver has prepared our way."

"Tomorrow we will move toward the land," Point Man said. "We are ready."

On the following day, the people formed their immense traveling procession and walked west to the winding river. Many of them thought this would be a brief journey for they knew that spring rains had swollen the river. The gently flowing river now had a raging current. They would have to wait for the waters to recede.

"Why are you downhearted?" asked Point Man as he met the elders that night.

"The river has blocked us," said the people.

"Tomorrow we cross," said Point Man.

"Impossible!" said some. Others remembered the stories of the past and said nothing.

"Impossibilities have never stopped Land-Giver from keeping his promises," reminded Point Man.

Soon after the sun rose, the procession approached the waters of the flood plain. Silver trumpets sounded. The keepers of the sanctuary carried the ark of mystery to the very edge of the waters—and kept walking. The flow diminished so that their sandals were set in mud but not even a puddle of water.

As the ark of mystery reached the river bank even the normal waters receded before it. The keepers of the Special Place who carried the ark on poles stopped at the middle of the stream bed as Point Man had instructed. Those who passed stared at the twin golden angels with outstretched wings sculpted on its lid. It almost seemed that those angel wings held back the waters.

All the People of the Promise crossed the Winding River that day.
All passed the ark with a feeling of great awe.
All wondered at the power of Land-Giver.

That night Point Man walked with Land-Giver alone. He wandered along the path that would take them to the great Fortress City. Suddenly the night was washed away by light. An angel twice as tall as a man with broad muscular shoulders stood in the road. His glowing face had the rugged look of a veteran warrior. His body was covered with silver armor and his powerful hands clutched the golden hilt of a flaming sword.

"Why do you stand between me and the mighty city?" asked Point Man.

"I have come to lead you if you have come to follow me. I am either your commander or your enemy."

"Whatever you command I will do. Wherever you lead I will go," said Point Man.

"Land-Giver has placed the Fortress City in your hands. You need only claim it."

"But the walls cannot be climbed. The gates cannot be forced."

"After seven days you will walk amid the rubble of the city and not one of your soldiers will die."

"This will indeed show the people that Land-Giver is infinite and eternal and all-powerful. It will not be we who do such a thing," responded Point Man after he listened to the angel's instructions.

"Nothing is high enough or heavy enough to block those who follow the ways of Land-Giver," said the angel in parting. "Obey my words and the city is yours."

An intense flash of light engulfed the angel; Point Man covered his eyes. It took minutes to grow accustomed to the darkness. He staggered to his feet. His mind raced through what he had seen and heard. Then he woke the keepers of the Special Place.

"We are ready," said the warriors.

"So is Land-Giver. It is time to advance."

"Half of the soldiers of the People of the Promise marched silently to the plain surrounding the Fortress City. To those on the walls it looked like the ranks would never stop coming over the rise. Then the great army formed just out of bow shot and began a slow and stately march around the perimeter of the defenses. At the front, keepers of the Special Place carried the ark of mystery. Before them walked seven keepers of the Special Place who continually blew rams' horns. The great army completed its circuit about the city then marched off over the rise and back to camp.

The king and those on the walls had expected an opening attack. They had gotten a procession. They were mystified.

Nothing was seen or heard from the People of the Promise until the following morning. Suddenly ranks of soldiers crested the same rise and formed the great army. Again the procession, led by the ark and the mournful cry of the rams' horns. Then the army disappeared over the rise once more.

"This is worse than a siege," breathed the king to one of his commanders as they watched the troops vanish.

For six days, early each morning, the warriors and the keepers made a single circle around the city. For six days, early each morning, the people inside trembled at the pulsating cadence of marching feet and the song of the rams' horns. The people plugged their ears and rushed to the ornate temple of the Shining One.

"Help us!" they cried. "Please save us."

But the temple was empty and there was no one to comfort their cries. During the first night, the priests of Shining One had fled the doomed city through secret underground passages. The people stood lost and alone before stone statues as they prayed for protection. Shining One heard their cries, but he could provide no protection.

High on the western wall, a long strip of scarlet linen fluttered from a high window. The two watchers smiled as they spotted the flag and pointed it out to the warriors. There, they reminded the warriors around them, was a sanctuary for the woman with long black locks. The Inn-Keeper sat peacefully behind that window with her father and mother and brothers and sisters.

They were calm in the midst of the city's terror.

They no longer looked to Shining One, for they had seen the anarchy of that path.

They looked out the window with excitement. They had become People of the Promise.

The sun rose bright above the mountains of the dawn on that seventh morning as the warriors started their silent march. Thousands of feet pounded the earth and then seven rams' horns tore the quiet. The city awoke with panic. Today the horns sounded twice as loud. The golden angels atop the ark of mystery sparkled with a magnificent presence that caused each heart within the walls to melt.

The warriors and the keepers circled the city once and then kept marching. The people inside the walls now knew this day was different. The fate of the city would be determined before the sun crossed the sky.

The warriors and the keepers circled the city a second time and a third and a fourth and a fifth. Tension mounted, and the people of the mighty city held each other and sobbed a tearless grief from hard hearts. They should feel confident inside the great walls. None felt snug and secure. The warriors and keepers circled a sixth time. Hopeless resignation paralyzed all who watched. Why wouldn't they charge? The warriors and keepers circled the mighty city a seventh time.

Then they stopped and their silence was deafening.

The people of the city trembled. Their eyes widened and throats tightened. Their breathing grew shallow.

Suddenly silver trumpets blasted with a force that rattled the walls and shattered the city's final fragments of courage. Children cried and women screamed and men cursed. Then half a million voices shouted in a rumbling unison: "LAND-GIVER REIGNS!"

The outer wall shifted and swayed. The massive structure groaned as its strength was tested. Foundation stones vibrated and cracked and crumbled. Stones from the top broke loose and fell. Warriors near the quivering walls ran back and those on the walls looked for a way down. Only a section of the western wall seemed undamaged.

Small cracks grew into large cracks and spread throughout the fortress. The heavy oak gates were wrenched apart as the walls loosened and flew open. None even ran to fill this fatal gap. The outer wall crumbled in an avalanche of broken rock that crashed into the inner wall, pulling it into the collapsing destruction. Clouds of dust choked those who had not been crushed by rock as an entire city suddenly came apart. The noise was deafening as stones collided and shattered into rubble. Through it all the People of the Promise stood still and listened and watched.

On the western wall a long strip of bright scarlet still fluttered from an intact portion of wall. The Inn-Keeper and her father and mother and brothers and sisters shut their ears to the screams of the city. Neither fear nor death had visited the room that sheltered them, and they could only guess the extent of what was occurring outside their doors. They were amazed at the power of Land-Giver.

As the clouds of dust began to settle, the trumpets blew one last blast. The soldiers pulled their swords and charged the city. They climbed the heaps of broken stone and searched the smoky desolation. There were only small skirmishes of opposition, so broken were the soldiers who knew their city and their lives were already lost.

In the center of the shattered city, at the once beautiful temple of Shining One, the defeated made a last stand. With swords and stones, they tried to stop the inevitable. Some soldiers of the People of the Promise said later that they were sure they had seen a great serpent amid the rubble. The snake crawled from beneath a broken statue and urged on his ragged followers. "They cannot hurt us. We will destroy them. Fight to the death."

The followers of Shining One fought until all of them lay dead in the temple courtyard.

Warriors collected the silver and gold that lay about in abundance and placed it before the ark as a tribute to Land-Giver. Point Man stopped them.

"Nothing is to be saved from this city—not so much as a coin or a scrap of fabric. We must take nothing because it is cursed in the sight of Land-Giver and any who keep it will be cursed.

But something was to be saved. The two watchers ran toward the west wall in search of the room from which the scarlet flew. When the Inn-Keeper saw the young men she opened her arms with a cry of joy. The three embraced and tears marked her face. Her family circled the watchers and gratitude was abundant.

The watchers escorted the Inn-Keeper and her family from the city and into the camp where they were clothed and fed and accepted. Already they felt they belonged.

That evening the warriors huddled around thousands of giant bonfires that lit the night in reds and yellows.

"The city is totally destroyed," said Point Man. "No one within the walls has survived except the Inn-Keeper and her family."

"And we had no injuries or losses," said one of the twelve leaders.

"Land-Giver did exactly as he said," announced another.

"He still is Promise-Keeper," said Point Man.

The twelve nodded in agreement and together affirmed: "Land-Giver is the source of every true victory."

The People of the Promise camped on the plain outside the great Fortress City and celebrated their commitment to Land-Giver and his to them.

MORAL INTEGRITY IS MORE PRECIOUS
AND LESS REPLACEABLE
THAN ANY BURIED TREASURE.

CHAPTER 8

THE SILVER AND GOLD

Silver and gold. Jewels and trinkets and fine cloth and coins. Large and small piles sparkled in the afternoon sun. One stumbled upon beautiful pieces lying about the ruins of the Fortress City. The warriors had collected it into piles for Land-Giver. But Point Man had stopped them, for everything in the Fortress City was under Land-Giver's curse. The men let it pile up in the buildings that still stood. Soon they would be burned. The flames would destroy much and melt the rest. One day perhaps another city would be built on this spot, and its founders would uncover an unexpected treasure.

It seems wasteful, thought more than one of the warriors. Wonder-ful things. And they could not take so much as a coin. The Inn-Keeper and her family could not bring any possessions except the clothes on their backs. Nothing could go even to the Special Place for Land-Giver.

Point Man assigned trusted warriors to guard the ruins that night for he knew the temptation was strong and knew the people needed to be protected from their own desires. Now the night was far gone; the fires burned low and a warrior shivered as he stood outside a building that would be put to the torch with the sun's rising. He avoided the dark doorway, but still he wrestled with the thought of so much wealth resting within reach. His feet kept bringing him back to the forbidden treasure room.

"You should at least look at it." whispered a voice in the darkness. The warrior went for the torch that burned nearby. Its light shined on the beautiful pattern of a serpent's skin. The snake had made a home among the piles of gold inside. The warrior had not seen Shining One before, but he knew who and what the serpent was.

"You will never see such baubles again," the snake continued.

"Away! Or taste my sword!" shouted the warrior. "This is not yours or mine. It belongs to Land-Giver to do with as he wishes."

"And he wishes to keep you from your fair share," said the snake in a tone of disgust. "No army has ever conquered a treasure city and then destroyed their own booty."

The snake slipped his head through a silver bangle. "Take a little touch. Other warriors have surely run their fingers over such riches. Perhaps some even slipped a treasure or two into their bags. If so, who was the wiser?"

No one was in sight when he stepped into the dark room and his torch gleamed on the horde about him. His fingers caressed a bar of refined gold. It still bore the shape of the smelter's mold.

"It's heavier than it looks," whispered the snake, "and very pure."

The warrior picked it up and weighed it in his hands. The bar glowed in the torchlight.

"How much do you suppose it's worth?" asked the snake.

"More than I will ever own," said the warrior. He was feeling rather sorry about his lowly birth.

"You could have a fine start in the new land with a single bar like this," agreed the snake.

"But it belongs to Land-Giver."

"And what will he do but destroy it? Years from now somebody will dig up potfuls of melted riches. They won't have put their life on the line for it as you did. You've earned at least a sample. Will he who holds stars in his hands begrudge a bit of earth metal?"

Almost unbidden, the hand slipped the bar into the leather bag slung at his waist.

"Now don't you want some silver?" asked the snake.

"No, nothing more!" spat the man.

"Look at all those silver coins—hundreds of them. Put a few in your bag."

The warrior looked at all the silver. He grabbed a fistful of coins and then another and another.

He avoided everyone as he returned to camp at daybreak. He dug a hole under the floor mats of his tent and buried his wealth. He buried it deep. Silver coins on the bottom and then the gold bar. Dirt to fill and a sleeping mat to cover. At last he could sleep.

But he didn't.

Days later Point Man called two more watchers to his side.

"Search out the highlands beyond the Fortress City. Journey west to the City of Death and spy out their strength."

The watchers filled small backpacks and walked west. The next day they climbed a ravine near the City of Death. This city was walled, but not so securely as the Fortress City. It was smaller. Its walls were not so high or wide nor its gates nearly so heavy.

The watchers counted the numbers of people and warriors. They studied its defenses and evaluated its preparations. Then they descended the ravine.

"With Land-Giver's help, a small force can destroy the city."

Under the cover of a new moon three thousand warriors silently climbed the ravine and surrounded the sleeping city. As dawn showed its first light, trumpets were blown and they surged toward the gates. But as the warriors moved forward, the gates flew open and thousands of soldiers rushed out with ferocious cries. They raced through the gate with shining swords. The warriors of Land-Giver slowed as fear gripped their hearts.

The surprise was bold and aggressive and bloody. Swords slashed through leather armor. Confusion shattered the attack. As more fell, the enemy increased its ferocity, for the soldiers were desperate not to die as had the people of the Fortress City. For the young and inexperienced soldiers of Point Man the fight was hopeless.

"Retreat!"

"Fall back!"

The warriors turned from the City of Death and fled as fast as fear could carry them. Their enemy pursued them for desperate miles before turning back to celebrate.

The warriors buried their dead.

And tended their wounded.

And cried out to Land-Giver: "Why did you abandon us?"

Point Man fell on his face before the Special Place. "You are our victory. Without you we are doomed. What have we done to cause you to leave our side?"

"You harbor a thief and a traitor," said Land-Giver. "Shining One has claimed the allegiance of one who has stolen from me."

"What was stolen?"

"Cursed silver and gold from the Fortress City."

"I feared someone might be weak. You asked a difficult thing from men who have nothing."

"Obedience is sometimes a difficult thing. Too soon Shining One has infiltrated and tested and found weakness. Now I ask another difficult thing. The traitor must die so my people will be reminded of who I am."

For the first time in the new land the mass of people was called before Point Man. The people stood before him full of questions.

"Someone has defiled the camp by taking cursed treasure from the Fortress City—treasure stolen from the hand of Land-Giver," announced Point Man.

No one spoke and no one stepped forward. The thief turned white and nearly fainted. He shifted his weight from foot to foot. The treasure was carefully hidden. He would not be found. But how had Point Man learned of the loss?

"Prepare the lots," said Point Man.

The keepers of the Special Place took the pieces of marked ivory to each elder and cast them down. A tribe was marked out. Clan leaders from the tribe were called forward. Now a guilty clan was identified. Family leaders slowly stepped forward. Embarrassment and concern showed on each face. Now a family was marked, and finally one frightened man stood alone.

Point Man quietly placed his hands on the shoulders of the sobbing warrior. "What have you done?" he asked softly.

"I knew I shouldn't listen to the serpent, but his words made so much sense. I was guarding the treasure and it was so tempting. I listened to him and followed. I couldn't turn away."

"Where have you hidden it?"

The thief lowered his head and spoke softly. "I buried it beneath the floor mat of my tent."

Soldiers soon returned and placed the stolen silver and gold before the elders. "You thought no one would see, but you acted in the very presence of Land-Giver. None of us ever acts outside his presence."

The thief now stood calmly and faced the elders and the people. His voice broke with each sentence, but the heralds passed his words back through the crowd. "I have betrayed the camp. I have caused the deaths of your fathers and husbands and sons. I have been a traitor to Land-Giver."

"You must face the penalty for what you have done. The camp must be cleansed," said Point Man as the elders stood around the man who knelt before them. "But it is not too late for you to take the hand of Land-Giver. You may still walk to his house if you follow him these last steps with a clean heart."

The thief and Point Man walked side by side with the elders and the men of the clan to a small valley. There they buried him and buried the doubly cursed silver and gold. When the people returned, they named the place the Valley of Sorrow.

Point Man swallowed hard, but the lump in his throat wouldn't move.

"Consequences seem cruel," said the wind.

Point Man nodded.

"Those who listen to Shining One bring death to all the people. The darkness that is not removed spreads."

Now a new note could be heard in the wind song: "Go to the City of Death. Be strong and courageous for I am your victory."

A small army and a large army set out. The small army moved ahead and hid itself near the city. The large army set out with the sun and marched toward the main gate.

The city's warriors saw the approaching army and bolstered their confidence with strong wine. This army was larger than the one before, but they had shown themselves far greater than these desert nomads. Again the main gate flew open and the enemy let out a yell and charged out with swinging swords. The warriors of Land-Giver slowed and seemed to give way once again, driven back but with little loss.

"Retreat!" came the call.

The warriors of Land-Giver again turned from the City of Death and fled. Every man of the city came out to give chase.

Soon the pursuing soldiers saw plumes of thick smoke rise from their city. Turning from the battle, they raced back. Before the city stood the small army. Now at their back was the large army. Trapped, they fought until all lay on the field.

The victory belonged to the people of Land-Giver. They danced and sang and thanked the one who holds the stars in his hands.

Not many days later all the people of Land-Giver moved from the river to the heights at the center of the new land. They came to keep their promise to General. With large uncut stones they built a tall monument of white stone that stood like sparkling snow against the bright blue sky. Then the people stood before this stone of remembrance and each made a vow.

"I will follow the words of Land-Giver with all my heart and with all my soul."

The people cheered.

The angels on the ark of mystery glowed.

A rainbow splashed across the sky.

LIES ARE DAGGERS;
WISDOM SEEKS THE FACTS
THAT BLUNT THE BLADE.

CHAPTER 9

THE LIE

Smoke from the City of Death rose dark and ominous. The people of the land watched fearfully for they saw how quickly the People of the Promise had captured the central highlands. Most frightened were the dwellers of the City on the Hill. They had no high walls or great army for they made their fortune by location. They were on the trade route to the Land of Pyramids and they lived a short march from the ruins of the City of Death. If the warriors turned south they would be next to fall. The leaders of the city gathered fearfully.

"Why don't we mount a surprise attack?" asked a young man.

"Look at how few we are and how many they are. Even if we were successful they would destroy us."

"What if we strengthen our walls and let them lay siege?" asked another.

"We don't have time to cut and haul and place the stone. And what good have walls done our dead neighbors?"

"I have heard it said that their Land-Giver is infinite and eternal and all-powerful," said the king sadly. "If that is true we cannot fight against him or his people."

"So perhaps we should join them," said an ancient, gray-bearded counselor.

The meeting burst into pandemonium.

"Impossible!"

"How could you even consider such a thing?"

"I'd rather die!"

"We follow Shining One!"

"Peace!" demanded the king. "How could we join them, Gray Beard?"

"We will make a treaty with them that pledges to honor their Land-Giver. We won't attack them. They won't attack us."

"What could possibly induce them to treaty with us?"

"They may not know it *is* us," said the old man with a sly smile.

A dusty and weary and bedraggled group of travelers was stopped by the outer guards of the camp.

"We have come to see the great warrior servant of Land-Giver who is called Point Man," said the leader of the group, a weathered and gray-bearded grandfather.

"At this hour Point Man walks with Land-Giver," said a commanding warrior. "Where are you from?"

"A distant country across the Fertile Crescent. Our king has heard of the might of the People of the Promise and the care of him who holds the stars in his hands. He has sent us to learn of Land-Giver and to seek the counsel of your great chief and to seek peace between our peoples."

"We have never heard of this people," snapped one of the elders as Point Man met with his council that morning. "They may be spies hired to learn our weaknesses."

"Then they will learn little," interrupted Point Man, "except that our strength is in Land-Giver. We will tell all of our enemies this secret. Let us meet these strangers before we treat them as enemies. Perhaps we will teach the glory of Land-Giver to a people willing to follow him."

"You may speak," Point Man told the travelers when they met in his tent.

"The story of your people has spread far beyond your vision. We know how the sea divided and the mountain spoke and the desert produced bread. We know Land-Giver is your victory against powerful armies. So even though many days separate us, our king sent us across the crescent to offer peace and friendship with such a wondrous people."

"Why haven't we heard of you before?" asked a suspicious elder.

"I am little surprised that you have not. That is how far we have come and it is the sign of our insignificance in your sight. On our journey we have worn out our clothes and shoes and drinking skins. We have no bread left but these dry and moldy crusts."

The bread crumbled in his hand. It looked barely edible.

"They do seem to have journeyed far," whispered an elder. "Land-Giver told General that he could make treaties with people who lived far enough away that they could not lead our people into the ways of Shining One."

The leaders discussed the travelers
and studied their clothing
and tasted their bread.

Then they ate a meal together and promised to defend as brothers and never to attack one another. They sealed their pledge with a binding oath to Land-Giver. But no one thought to ask Land-Giver what they should do and he was not happy.

"What you have done was very foolish," said the wife of one of the twelve.

"We listened to the travelers and studied their situation," said the husband. "We know what we're doing."

"However wise you are, you should have sought Land-Giver's counsel."

Point Man yelled at the sky, "Why didn't we seek your words?"

Warriors of the Land-Giver had marched to the City on the Hill and surrounded it. Point Man had arranged his force to attack. It promised to be a brief battle. They knew how to take cities now and this one had few soldiers and poor defenses. It was a notorious city of the followers of Shining One.

The gate opened. Instead of soldiers issuing forth, a single man walked fearlessly out to the army. Point Man recognized the old face with weathered beard. A bad feeling filled his belly.

The ancient man was brought before him.

"My friends, why have you come with implements of war as if you are attacking the city of your allies and servants? Let us instead gather for feasting."

The truth was painfully clear.

"Let's attack their gate and burn their homes," said the commanding warrior.

"No," said Point Man. "We will keep our promise made in the name of Land-Giver."

"But they lied. It was a treaty made in bad faith."

Point Man ignored the angry commander and faced the gray-bearded man. "Take me to your king," he said simply.

Point Man entered the city
and the king's lavish house
and a large room prepared for a feast.
The aroma was sweet and the tables overflowed.

"We have waited for you, good master," said the small round man in a long purple robe. "Bring all your commanding warriors and let us sample the fruit of your new land."

"Why did you lie to us?" Point Man asked, ignoring the lavish setting.

"You must know the answer to that. No army can stand before the warriors of Land-Giver. Certainly not our meager forces. We did not want to die. And so we have pledged our lives to you."

"We will not destroy you or your city, but you and your children and your children's children will be our servants. From this point forward you will be woodcutters and water carriers. You will serve us and we will protect you so long as you do not draw our people toward Shining One."

"Thank you for your mercy," said the king. "Now please invite your men and let us eat together."

Warriors watched the dances of the daughters of the city that night. Land-Giver looked in sorrow as the snake watched the celebration. One of the cities of Shining One had been spared.

When the king of the City of Palms heard of the peace treaty, he was angry and alarmed. He immediately called a meeting of the five kings, representing the land's great cities.

"The People of the Promise are destroying us one at a time. Now one of our own cities has joined them. The only answer is to unite and attack them all at the time and place we choose," he proclaimed.

"If all five of us join our armies, we can crush them," said a second king.

"Look what they did to the Fortress City and the City of Death," said another.

"Neither acted wisely," said the king of the city. "We will learn from their errors."

"Their warriors follow Land-Giver."

"And we follow Shining One. Surely he is as great as their Defender. We will strike first and show them we aren't afraid."

The five kings decided to open their battle with an attack on the City on the Hill. This would punish the city for making peace and entice the enemy to move into a trap they would set.

The army of the five kings lay siege to the City on the Hill. They encircled the walls and assaulted the gates. But they allowed a quick and courageous messenger to escape past their lines.

"Please save us," begged the messenger to Point Man. "We are your servants and without your help we are lost. The five kings to the south have besieged us and we cannot stand."

"Land-Giver shall be your protection," said Point Man.

Point Man led his army to the City on the Hill. Through the night they marched, and before the sun colored the Mountains of the Dawn, their great army was prepared to battle the five kings. The kings had not expected such speed and were taken by surprise. Many still slept as warriors of the People of the Promise rushed their camp. They awoke in panic as their enemy caught them without swords or shields. Many of the kings' soldiers were struck down near their own tents. The rest fled south toward the City of Palms. But before they reached their refuge, Land-Giver opened up the clouds against them. Hail fell, killing more than had been struck by Point Man's attack.

As the storm ended, Point Man circled the fleeing army and blocked the road to the City of Palms. Now they were surrounded and fought valiantly. Sword struck sword until the warriors of Land-Giver were exhausted.

Point Man saw that the strength of his warriors was weakening and the day was fading. "If the enemy holds on until nightfall they will escape to their refuge," Point Man called out to Land-Giver, "Hold back the night until our battle is won."

A gentle wind blew against Point Man's face and whispered, "The battle is yours."

Fighting continued with renewed fervency and the sun stopped its descent to the horizon. The soldiers of the five kings realized that all of nature and even the sun had turned against them. One by one they fell until all lay breathless. Only then did the sun slip toward the great sea. Throughout the battle the five kings could not be found. Some said they escaped to the City of Palms; others said they'd gone north to get reinforcements from the cities surrounding the stormy sea.

A week later watchers returned to report that the kings had been seen. They were hidden in a cave. Soldiers surrounded the cave and within a few days they returned with five ragged-looking kings.

"Why do you fight Land-Giver?" asked Point Man.

The kings stood silent.

"Why do you follow the ways of the Shining One?"

Again the kings stood silent.

"These men are dangerous and defiant," said Point Man to his warriors. "But no one can battle Land-Giver and expect to win. This is what the one above all things will do to any who keep you from the land he has promised."

And the five were struck down.

Without the five kings and their armies the southern lands could not hope to stand against the People of the Promise. Warriors of Land-Giver marched from city to city until they had overcome everything south of the City on the Hill.

"Now we must march north and the land will be ours." He paused and looked beyond the sky. "Land-Giver is our victory."

CHAPTER 10

THE PLACE OF PEACE

T his cannot be. All the cities of the central highlands? All the cities of the southern hills?"

"All are fallen between the Fortress City and the desert's edge. Those who did not flee are dead."

The king of the Double City would not have believed, but he had seen the refugees. Daily they passed through, bound for—anywhere—beyond the reach of the People of the Promise. Few asked to stay. "It is no safer here," they said. "You should leave too."

Many did.

The king knew that many People of the Promise had invaded from the Plains of Comfort. They were shepherds and desert dwellers. They were former slaves if the stories be true. How could all of the land be in peril?

He turned to the messenger. "What do they want? What bargain will they make to pass us by?"

"No bargains. They have a treaty with the City on the Hill. They will consider no other. They say this is their land—all of it—given to them long ago. They have returned to claim it."

"If it was theirs long ago, it is not now," said the king. "Who do they think gave them our homes?"

"They call him Land-Giver," said the messenger. "They say he alone holds the stars in his hands."

"I know something of this ancient enemy of Shining One. Our peoples have always fought one another. Now we fight once more. The kingdoms of the north have nothing to fear if we will act as one."

"I would still fear. None of the people of the south stood before Land-Giver's followers."

"Fear overcame them. Shining One also promises victory to *his* followers," said the king. "We shall see who keeps promises."

Urgent messages issued from the gates of the Double City. Fourteen kings of the north responded. All knew the threat well. They knew Point Man now aimed his slings and javelins and swords northward. War would come, war to the death—merciless and bloody and perhaps hopeless.

So they came, every man.

The king was amazed at their numbers. The kings of the south had assembled no such force. Thousands and thousands and more thousands of men. They were unafraid and fighting for home and family. Such an army could not be defeated. "Let us see what Land-Giver can do now." These armies were well-equipped for battle:

A thousand chariots with wheels and plating of iron.

More war stallions than had ever stood side by side.

Swords and shields of hardest metals.

It was a vast sea, thought the two scouts who watched the camps of the kings gather in a lush green valley near the Stormy Sea.

"As many as we have, they have far more," the two told Point Man in awed voices. "If it is possible to keep us from taking the land, this is the army that can do it."

"No one can keep us from what Land-Giver promises," said Point Man. "Tomorrow we will go to them before they have time to be ready. Land-Giver has brought our remaining enemies together. This battle will make his name known over all the blue planet, for we can stand before any enemy if Land-Giver holds our shields and swings our swords."

The watchers moved through the land noting the well-worn roadways and the narrow mountain trails. Such information prepared Point Man. He divided his army, sending his slower soldiers and wagons over better roads, his quick younger soldiers came by the harder ways. They would meet on both flanks of the great plain where the enemy gathered. He could move faster in smaller numbers without fear of an ambush. He knew where his enemies were and where they were going.

Three days the soldiers pressed on with only short rests. The watchers reported on the locations of other parts of the army. So they reached their objectives at about the same time and quickly surrounded the plain on which their enemies gathered. Among those armies all was in disarray. They were not ready. They had no plan. How could so many have come so far so quickly and hold such excellent strategic position?

Keepers of the Special Place built a simple stone altar and sacrificed a spotless newborn lamb. The sweet smoke drifted beyond the sky and the wind whispered, "Be strong and courageous."

Silver and ram's horn trumpets seemed to sound all around when the attack was announced. A tidal wave of warriors swept toward the hastily arranged defenders. The enemy was in chaos.

Kings yelled conflicting commands.

Warriors wondered whether to fight or flee.

Well-laid strategies were forgotten.

Chariots could not find the space to maneuver. Troops with slings concentrated their stones on the horsemen. Armies clogged one another's paths of escape and regrouping.

This day blood flowed more freely than had ever soaked into the land. The northern armies fell into fatal confusion. Commanders stood tall and tried to rally their men but were soon spotted and cut down. Those who could find their way from the field of battle fled into the waiting arms of Land-Giver's army.

Small nations ceased to exist that day. Widows and orphans would soon leave their city walls behind and run to mountain caves or other lands. Rare were the old men who could tell village children how they had once fought against the warriors of Land-Giver and survived. Not one of the kings would tell their stories.

Shining One had lost the land at least for a time. He worried little about all who had fallen. More would be found—many of them from the winning side in this battle. Other battles remained to be won and lost.

But now the soldiers of the People of the Promise returned to their families and their cheers resounded through valleys and off hills. The battle was won; the land lay empty to claim. Most of the cities that had followed Shining One were destroyed. Parts of the highlands remained unconquered and received survivors.

Point Man gathered the elders. Three men were chosen from each tribe to survey and explore and map. They studied the land from the edge of the southern desert to the headwaters of the Winding River. They described valleys and ravines and rivers. Much was learned about the land. Each tribe and clan and family was given the territory it had been allotted.

Horns sounded as the ark of mystery passed through the camp. The Special Place also needed a place to rest. The elders and keepers of the Special Place would follow the wind until it stopped. That would be the home of the golden angels with outstretched wings. Many joined the procession following the beautiful ark. It was such a holiday. People danced and sang and gave thanks to Land-Giver. There was plenty to eat in untended fields they passed. The ark wandered that day across the central highlands. As the shadows grew long the wind died in a valley surrounded by quiet hills thick with timber. The keepers set down the ark and the angels glowed in the final hours of light. "This is my new home," whispered the wind.

Hundreds of torches lit the valley as the keepers raised the Special Place and carried the ark into the solitude of the Most Hallowed Chamber. When Land-Giver rested between the golden angels all the people sensed his presence. Spotless lambs were sacrificed in the last twilight.

The next morning, as the trees glittered with a touch of dew and the birds sang a gentle wake-up tune, Point Man walked with Land-Giver.

"The land has been conquered for now, though Shining One's people remain and more will come," said the wind. "But today is a joyful time. Send those who remain with you to their own lands, but tell them to return often to this place."

"Is my work finished?"

"I have reserved for you a city. Go there and enjoy the land but also be a counselor and friend to all the people who will look to you. Much remains to do and you will need to remember to walk with me each day."

"How could I forget to walk with the one who lives beyond the sky and holds the stars in his hands?"

As the sun touched the roof of the sky the people gathered before the Special Place. It was a beautiful day and a beautiful place—so different from the desert wastes where this Special Place had stood.

Here trees grew straight and true and abundant.

Here small mountains rose above while wheat and barley waved below.

Here people with broken hearts could walk with Land-Giver.

In sadness and joy, old friends parted and those who remained from each of the twelve tribes turned toward their scattered homes. Yet none forgot the desert or the battlefield or the valley. Finally the ark rested in a Place of Peace and the land could begin to heal. Each spring and summer and fall men of every clan and family would stand before the Special Place and thank Land-Giver. They would tell their children and grandchildren of the jewel in the center of their land where the ark of mystery glowed in the Most Hallowed Chamber and reflected a glimpse of Land-Giver's glory.

Many of the people who stood in the valley would see Point Man once more, years later, when he called the elders of the tribes together to hear his final words. Many came and stood in the shade of oaks not far from the tall white monument rock they had built years before.

"Be strong and courageous," said Point Man. "Cling to Land-Giver and beware of Shining One. You know his people remain all around, calling us toward anarchy. Do not listen to their words or fall into their snares or marry their fair ones. If you do, they will turn your hearts from your commitment. They will not become like you. You will become like them."

The people nodded in agreement and promised.

"Remember all that has happened. Let no word be lost of the journals of General and tell your children all you have seen. Proclaim everywhere you go that Land-Giver is our victory. He is our shield and sword in battle. He is our peace in times of calm or storm.

"When you feel tempted or confused or fearful, remember what you promised on the Plains of Comfort and be true to your word."

The leaders renewed their vow to Land-Giver. That night they sat around many fires telling the stories of Delta King and the night of nights, the mountain and the morning bread, the sorcerer and the mighty Fortress City.

The next morning, Point Man watched the people fade into the distance as they went to their homes and families and fields. Not many days later he closed his eyes. His body felt light and his mind clear. The wind whispered more gently than ever before. Point Man held out his hand and Land-Giver lifted him from his ancient warrior body. The two greeted each other and walked beyond the sky as the scent of eternity once more lingered over the land.

But so few could catch its scent.

EPILOGUE

Words ceased.

The man with a hundred wrinkles disappeared into the shadows. The people stared at the final flickers of the once grand fire, and an indescribable calm blanketed the group. Sweet fragrance drifted through the circle and suddenly the difficulties of life were a different color.

"Can you smell it?" the girl child asked her mother.

"Yes," the mother said with a smile. "I smell it, though it is hard to separate from the other smells and few notice its freshness."

"What is its name?"

"The scent of eternity."

The girl child smiled. "I should have guessed. It's wonderful."

All was quiet.

"May I ask another question?"

"Yes, my little one. Questions are good."

"Where is the Place of Peace?" asked the girl.

"Long ago it was in the highlands, but it is no longer there."

"Where is it now?"

The mother gently stroked the child's frizzled hair. Then she picked her daughter up and hugged her close.

"If you walk with Land-Giver, the Place of Peace is anywhere you are, even where it isn't peaceful."

"How can that be?"

"You carry it here," the mother said tapping the little head.

"You also carry it here," she said again, pointing to the little heart.

"That's what I thought," said the girl with a smile that made her eyes twinkle.

PART 3
PEOPLE-BUILDER

TABLE OF CONTENTS
PEOPLE-BUILDER

PROLOGUE

Rain greened the pasture land. So it was a cheerful evening for the men as they considered a plumper flock and less stress on lambing ewes. They also cast glances at the young boy who had suddenly become a man before their eyes. A marriage had been arranged. Now the prospective groom tried to ignore the women who were busily planning the upcoming marriage feast. Children played a game with rounded stones.

Times of joy.

Marrying, birthing, growing times.

People times.

The man with a hundred wrinkles tugged at his beard as he watched a community. He thought of other communities and times when harmony gave way to hostility.

It reminded the old man of stories about the blessing of having one another. He got slowly to his feet and stepped into the circle of fire glow.

Several older women had carefully built and tended the crackling blaze of fig and olive branches. Once again the people became expectantly quiet. The old man stood quietly for long moments. The people leaned toward the warm and comforting fire as eerie shadows danced in the desert beyond. It was late and the world was alive with the sounds of night animals. Some sounds were friendly, some threatening. A jackal made its jagged cry.

But that was out there, away from the community of the circle.

The old man turned his back to the fire and faced the eager listeners.

He had told a story for each night in this cycle of the moon. Some made one think. Some were exciting. Some were sad.

Ten stories he would now begin to tell. Ten stories about community and the one who builds a community. Ten stories would remind the people of ten leaders who had shaped the New Land. Most of those around the fire had heard the stories before, but words are too often forgotten.

The storyteller closed his eyes, then opened them and raised his hand. "Listen!"

A lion roared in the distance, sending a shiver through the people, more of curiosity than fear. But was it a lion they had heard? There were few lions about these days. Perhaps it was a voice of the past become present. Perhaps it was the voice of People-Builder building his people.

A NEW APPROACH CAN TOPPLE
AN OLD OBSTACLE IF ONE IS
WILLING TO GIVE IT A TRY.

CHAPTER 1

THE LION

T he land is in trouble," said the wind.

"I know," said Point Man's best friend. "Even the Valley of Apples is under attack. We did not destroy all who lived here before us. We thought we had done enough. We were wrong. Now they want to reclaim their land."

"The land belongs to my people—so long as they walk with me. But already they hesitate. They are not walking with me; they are not following my steps."

"Is that why there are new battles?" asked Companion.

"As long as Shining One remains, there will be new battles. But only as long as my people walk with me will there be new victories."

Companion waited for the voice of Land-Giver to continue. Would he turn from them? Then the wind spoke comfortingly:

"When the time is right. . .

"When my people come to the Place of Peace. . .

"When they look to the highlands. . .

"Then I will call and arm and send them into battle. Then I will be their victory."

"General and Point Man are no longer among us. Soon I will be gone. When will you give us new leaders?"

"When the time is right," repeated the voice.

The followers of Shining One who had run to other lands returned. Others slipped from their hiding caves and gathered in the thick forests. They were given arms by those who feared and hated the People of the Promise.

Now they came suddenly from the hills. They circled unaware towns and killed the people. Valley by valley and hill by hill—slowly they began to regain the land.

Companion wanted to rest, but he gathered an army, and with the help of Land-Giver forced back the raiders.

"You cannot have what Land-Giver has taken from you!" he yelled at his enemy. He recaptured all of the towns.

All the towns but one: the City of Books.

The followers of Shining One made this their strongest fortress. They held this city firmly. Companion attacked. He attacked again and again. The City of Books did not fall.

"I am old and tired and ready to join Point Man," Companion told the warriors. "I cannot fight as a young man and this city is too strong for me.

"But in my old age I took a wife and she gave birth to a daughter. My youngest daughter has grown into a beautiful woman.

"The man who leads this people to victory—to that man I give in marriage my youngest daughter."

The troops silently measured themselves against the challenge given. Then a voice rang out.

"I will give you the city!"

Companion looked up, for this voice he knew. It was his nephew, a young man barely tried in battle. "You cannot take the city. You are too young," he said dismissively.

"Young I am," said Nephew. "And I am strong and courageous and I walk with Land-Giver. For I know that no man has the strength to give you the city. Land-Giver alone is our victory."

Companion smiled at his nephew's wisdom.

"You have spoken well. I will not stop you."

It was the night of the full moon when Nephew gathered a thousand warriors in the Valley of Apples. These were hand-picked men—strong with sharp swords and the desire for victory.

"Land-Giver gave us this land!" shouted Nephew. "He said it is ours and we will keep it."

In the nearby city they heard the shout of agreement. It echoed off the hills and made Companion tremble with excitement.

The sun's first light warmed a thousand backs standing straight before the city. As the sun touched the roof of the sky, they charged the gate and wall; their fierceness melted the hearts of the defenders. Blow upon blow battered the gate. Arrow after arrow pierced those who showed themselves.

Now the strong wood shuddered

then cracked

then crashed!

Warriors burst through and the city was theirs before the sun dropped from view.

Companion embraced his nephew. "You are young. But you have strength and courage and you walk with Land-Giver. You are a young lion with a mighty roar."

From that day forward he was known as Lion.

The Valley of Apples was full of pink and white blossoms that sparkled in the afternoon sun when Lion gave his promise to his bride. Surely this was the most beautiful of the blue planet's places, and he knew he looked into the eyes of one of Land-Giver's treasures. She was more to be valued than any victory he might ever win.

Companion gave his daughter a large field in the middle of the valley. It was fed by two clear springs. Lion and his bride worked the land and raised children and walked with Land-Giver. Companion lived nearby. Three times each year he saddled his donkey and journeyed a few days north with Lion. There they gave thanks and sacrificed a spotless lamb at the Place of Peace. But as the years passed, fewer men and women stood with them before the Special Place.

"What has happened to the People of the Promise?" asked Lion as they watched the smoke go up from their sacrifice to Land-Giver.

"They have lost their way," admitted Companion. "Point Man gave directions, but the words faded. Summers have passed, and I am the last of the leaders to breathe who heard Point Man's warnings."

"What were Point Man's warnings?"

"To beware of the followers of Shining One. To shut out their words and avoid their snares and not look upon their fair ones. But a new generation listens and is ensnared and takes their beautiful ones as wives. They have turned their backs on Land-Giver."

"What can we do?"

"I can do no more," said Companion in a tired voice. "I have few days left. You are the future, if you listen to his words and continue to walk in his ways."

As the two crossed over into the Valley of Apples, Companion gasped and slid from his donkey. Lion rushed to his side, but the old one's heart was still.

"Companion has passed beyond the sky," whispered the wind. "Now you are my people's leader."

"But your people won't be led. They follow Shining One and wish anarchy."

"That is true for now," said the wind. "But one day soon they will turn to me and I will ask you to lead my people. Meanwhile work the land and love your wife and walk with me."

"I will do whatever you ask," replied Lion.

"Then call me by my new name. In the beginning I came as Garden-Maker and Promise-Keeper. General called me Bondage-Breaker. Point Man knew me as Land-Giver. But you and those who come after you will know me as People-Builder. For I am building my people."

Years passed. The People of the Promise trampled on the ten special words that had been written on stone tablets at the mountain.

They were deaf to People-Builder's word and their hearts grew hard.

They lied and stole and murdered.

They did whatever Shining One asked until he poisoned their land with their anarchy and raised a stench before People-Builder.

The one above all things turned his back upon those who no longer cared. He opened the northern boundary of the New Land and allowed a cruel enemy to slash and beat and plunder its way across the countryside. Warriors gathered to resist but they knew no leader. Without People-Builder as their sword and shield there were no victories. They fell on the field by thousands and all who were left fled to caves. Lion watched and waited but continued to work his land. People-Builder had not yet called him.

Through eight endless summers that burned hot.

Difficult hard-working years of oppression and curse.

Days of restless sorrow and hopeless yearning.

Disappointment grew toward Shining One as the people recognized the emptiness and deception of his promises. He was not infinite nor eternal nor all-powerful. The people began to come a few at a time to the Place of Peace. They spoke with the keepers of the Special Place.

"Where is the one who holds the stars in his hands?" they asked.

"Waiting."

"For what does he wait?"

"For his people to call his name and walk his ways."

"But we have forgotten how. And we have acted so wickedly that he will never return."

The keepers pointed to the sky. Rain mixed with sun and a bright colored arch stretched above the hills. The people grew silent. Here was a message, if only they knew its meaning.

"He is always close," said the keepers, "and he will always care."

The people feared that these words could not be true.

"Turn toward him whose name is People-Builder," continued the keepers. "Call his name, and he will come. Turn toward him, and he will be your victory once more."

Messengers spread the promise of the rainbow throughout the land and all the people were called to the Place of Peace. Thousands of men made the journey. Within a week, a great throng of men stood before the Special Place. Each held a spotless newborn lamb to be sacrificed to People-Builder.

"We were foolish," said a muscular man with long hair. "We turned our backs away from the one who can do all and followed the one who can do nothing."

The snake coiled by a nearby rock and raised his head. His eyes glowed with hatred. His hissed threat of vengeance made angels shudder. Someone threw a stone at the serpent and it slithered back to its hole.

"Please bring a leader who can save us from our enemy," continued the muscular man.

"I have chosen," boomed a voice from the Most Hallowed Chamber. "He walks with me through the hill country near the Valley of Apples. He has waited many seasons for my people to seek me. He will lead you to victory."

When Lion stood before the men, they cheered and raised their weapons. The sweet aroma of thousands of sacrifices drifted toward People-Builder. Then Lion roared.

"Grasp your swords.

"Pick up your shields.

"Let us chase the enemy from our soil."

The ease of the last years had made the enemy army smug. They were totally unprepared for an army to surge from the Place of Peace. In a single cycle of the moon the northern invaders were forced to withdraw to their homeland with great loss of life. And few among the People of the Promise had dead to mourn.

The men had proved that the People of the Promise were still great warriors.

But to their credit, they took none of the glory.

"People-Builder is our victory!" shouted the warriors. "And Lion is our leader."

For many summers the land rested and Lion ruled and the people walked the ways of People-Builder.

CHAPTER 2

OUTSIDER

When Lion passed from the blue planet, something died inside the People of the Promise. They forgot their vows to People-Builder. Few visited the Place of Peace. Fewer walked with the one who holds stars in his hands.

Turmoil stirred the New Land; the king of the plains saw opportunity and his army crossed the Winding River. The People of the Promise had neither army nor governor.

No one called for People-Builder to be their sword and shield.

No one looked to the highlands for help.

No one remembered the source of all victory.

The People of the Promise became servants of the Plains People. Half of all the newborn lambs were claimed by the invaders with half of every harvest. Survival became difficult. And then the rain stopped.

Crops wilted and dried up.

Animals died.

The people grew thin.

"It must be the worst famine since the days of Merchant," thought the friendly man with a stubbly gray beard who stood at the gate to the City of Hope. Gatekeeper had fought beside Lion, and he had married a kind-hearted woman. Life was good. But his sons were born pale and weak and sickly. Now he feared for them.

So Gatekeeper left the gate. He left the City of Hope and the New Land. He took his family across the Plains of Comfort to the plateau of the Plains People. Here the sons grew stronger, but one day powerful pains ripped through the father's arm and chest. As he closed his tired eyes, the breath left his body. The sons gently laid their father in a cave tomb.

They married women of the plains, and for ten summers they were happy until a sickness settled over the land.

"These people are under People-Builder's judgment," said Gatekeeper's wife. "It is time to return to the City of Hope."

"This is our home," insisted her sons. "We will not go."

Within a cycle of the moon, the sickness was in the young men. In another cycle both lay beside their father.

Her eyes red and swollen, Gatekeeper's wife embraced her sons' wives.

"My husband and I were wrong to leave our people and now I have buried my men in a foreign country. I must say good-bye, my daughters. Go back to the homes of your parents."

The younger kissed her mother-in-law good-bye.

"My few belongings are easily gathered," the older said simply and firmly.

"Your place is here. There is no future at my side," said the widow.

"My mother, the future I care to live is with you."

"I go where People-Builder calls me," said Gatekeeper's wife. "He calls me back to the City of Hope."

"Where you go, I go. Where you rest, I rest," said the daughter-in-law.

There was no more to be said.

The road was long and dusty and silent. At last the two entered the gate where Gatekeeper had welcomed weary travelers. And many saw them arrive.

"Did you hear? The wife of Gatekeeper has returned."

"She looks so old and tired."

"Where is her husband? What has become of her sons?"

"She seems alone but for a Plains woman."

A neighbor spat.

"She should leave dogs where she finds them."

As friends gathered around Gatekeeper's wife, a silent young woman with downcast eyes stood behind her mother-in-law.

"I have returned forsaken but for my daughter," said Gatekeeper's wife. "She has come to be one of us."

People went away quiet and sullen.

"Outsider!"

"Daughter of our oppressor!"

"May People-Builder drop a rock on her head. I will hold it for him."

Gatekeeper's wife heard none of this, but she saw the hatred. At least they had a home. People-Builder had given the land to families and it remained in their hands. The relatives of Gatekeeper were obliged to give back his family home.

The women had little food and no friends, but People-Builder had given the law of widows. At harvest the workmen did not gather all the grain stalks. Widows followed, gathering grain to sustain them. No widow or orphan could be turned away—not even hated outsiders.

On the first day of barley harvest, Outsider went early to a large field. She bent her back and did not stop when the sun climbed the sky.

The landowner noticed her when he came to oversee the work.

"I thought I knew the gatherers. Who is that young woman?" he asked.

"Look at her skin and hair. She is an outsider—daughter-in-law of Gatekeeper's wife."

"So this is the terrible enemy everyone fears," laughed the landowner. He went to the outsider and held out his water skin.

"Sir, I am unworthy of your kindness."

"If you do not stop you will be ill. Take shelter in the shade of my trees. Drink of my water jars. If anyone bothers you, come to me."

"Don't you know who I am?" Outsider asked a little bitterly.

"I know you are a steadfast daughter to Gatekeeper's dear wife. I know you have left behind all to follow People-Builder. Nothing else do I need to know."

As the workers took their rest in the heat of the day, Outsider worked. When the air cooled, workers gathered for the harvest meal. Large tables were set beneath the ancient oaks with bread and cheese and fruit.

Landowner went to Outsider.

"You have worked through the heat of the day. You will do your mother-in-law no good if you die. Join us; we have plenty."

"Your people do not want me eating their food."

"None will speak unkindly to my guest."

There were curious glances but hard work earned respect. Outsider gathered until the last light faded. By torchlight she took her place with the other women. She beat the stalks to dislodge the grain. She trod the grain to knock off the husks and tossed it up to let the evening breeze blow away the chaff. The kernels were collected in one basket and the straw was bundled to use for bedding.

As she prepared to return home, Landowner set a bag of cleaned grain at the tired woman's side.

"Take this to Gatekeeper's wife," he said with concern. "And come back tomorrow. You will be welcome and safe in my fields."

Her mother-in-law could hardly believe the weight of grain her daughter-in-law carried. "Where did you work?"

"In the fields of a gentle landowner near the city walls, a kind man."

"That is my husband's cousin—protector of our clan. He is grandson of a foreign woman—Inn-keeper! People-Builder led you to that field."

Outsider followed Landowner's workers over his fields through the barley and wheat harvests. Her arms were hard and strong and even darker from the sun. She glowed with health.

"Has the landowner continued to be kind?" asked Gatekeeper's wife.

"All of his men are kind and he especially."

"His wife died years ago. He is surely ready to marry again. He is older, but you will not find a better man."

"He is a very good man. But I have no father or brother to go to him."

The old woman sat silently then spoke again: "Let People-Builder be your father."

"Let him offer me in marriage?"

"The harvest is in but not sold and stored. Landowner will trust no one to protect his grain from thieves. He guards it alone through the night. Go to him tonight and claim your right to the law of the brother."

It was Landowner's favorite time. He spread blankets over the soft grain. At the end of harvest, the cushioned bed gave satisfying rest after a good meal and sweet wine. But though he dozed, an inner sense was alert.

Someone was there in the blackness. He was certain of it.

"Who are you?"

"Outsider," came a soft and shy and hesitant reply. "I have come to ask for your protection. I am a widow without children. Will you fulfill the law of the brother?"

People-Builder had given the law of the brother to protect young widows. If a husband died and there were no children, an unmarried brother or another relative married the widow. Their first child would carry on the name and receive the inheritance of the dead man.

That law raced through the man's mind as he reached for a small torch. Light reflected faintly on black hair and shining eyes.

"You are a beautiful woman with great heart and character," he said. "Young men will offer you marriage. You need not look to one who has seen so many harvests."

"Sir, I am honored that you see value in me. I also look for integrity and gentleness and a kind heart. You have these in abundance. No husband could make me happier."

The man nearly cried. Here was a blessing he had never thought to receive.

"The law of the brother demands that the closest relative fulfill the obligation. I am not your husband's closest relative."

"Then you cannot marry me?"

"We shall see, if you are sure of your willingness. I will find a good husband to protect you and Gatekeeper's widow."

"I would prefer you, for I think you are a man of great worth."

"And I know you are a woman of great worth."

With Landowner's blanket about her shoulders, she lay at his feet and slept peacefully. Before the first light colored the mountains of the dawn, she slipped silently away.

The merchants chatted with a knot of men near the city gate. There was a little business and more gossip. Here were the city elders, and Landowner leaned against the wall waiting. He waved to a prosperous looking merchant across the busy market place.

When he had the elders' attention, he began:

"Fathers, you know that Gatekeeper and his sons are dead and none carries on their name. But a young widow could bear a child to that line."

Landowner turned to the merchant. "She claims the law of the brother. I have pledged that she will marry you, her closest relative, or I will fulfill the law."

The merchant was caught unawares. He considered the ramifications.

"I have built my fortune to one day pass to a son. What you ask could jeopardize that. The firstborn would belong to the line of Gatekeeper. And why should the daughter of our enemy have the right to this law?"

"Lest you forget, we too are born to the line of an outsider who turned from Shining One," said Landowner.

"You are right. But if you are willing to fulfill the law, I renounce my responsibility."

"Then listen to me, elders of the City of Hope," said the landowner loudly and solemnly. "You have heard that the duty of the brother falls to me. I declare that I take Outsider as my wife so that the children of Gatekeeper will go on forever."

Much of the city hastily gathered beneath the ancient oaks of Landowner's large barley field to hear the vows of fidelity. Now Outsider was one of them. She radiated stunning beauty as she stood before her protector with modesty and elegance.

They joined hands.

They joined lives.

They joined futures.

A fragrant breeze drifted through the trees. "You are greatly blessed," whispered the breeze. "From your line will come kings."

A summer later she held a baby to her breast and thanked People-Builder for his goodness.

"Where you go, I go," she whispered softly as she looked beyond the sky. "Where you rest, I rest."

WEAKNESS,
ATTACHED TO A HUMBLE HEART,
CAN BECOME ONE'S
GREATEST STRENGTH.

CHAPTER 3

LEFT HAND

He was born in the year Lion left the blue planet. As a child, he watched the misery of his village after the Plains People crossed the Winding River and conquered the central highlands. He saw the enemy tents amid the ruins of the Fortress City.

New walls rose from fallen stone.

Public buildings rose from rubble.

A grand palace rose from Shining One's ruined temple.

The boy tended his father's flocks in the hills. He stayed to himself. Other children took advantage of his small size. They laughed at him when he said that he walked with People-Builder. What seemed most unfair was that they laughed because he did not favor his right hand. The boy tried to train his right hand, but it was clumsy. He became self-conscious, which made him more clumsy. Some said use of the left hand over the right was a defect, others called it a curse. People avoided him and whispered until he begged his parents to let him stay in the hills with the flocks, though he was young for that responsibility.

In the hills, he walked every morning at the sun's first light with People-Builder. One day the wind whispered, "You will be a great warrior and your left hand will free your people from their enemy."

So he worked hard to make that left arm muscular and the hand strong. Then one day, as he shepherded his father's flocks near the old Fortress City, he saw the king of the Plains People come through the gates surrounded by soldiers in fine uniforms.

What struck the boy about the king was not all the finery. He had never seen anyone so amazingly round. The enemy king was very strong, but he also was very large around the middle. He was a shrewd leader who was greatly respected by his people.

Once a year the people of the New Land brought the king tribute: Great flocks of young sheep were herded toward the city and wooden carts brought in half of the grain harvest. When he was older, the young man drove spring lambs into the pens near the rebuilt walls of the Fortress City for the king. It angered him for he knew that the king was getting richer and his own people grew poorer. It seemed that the great king was getting larger and rounder as the People of the Promise were ill-fed and thin.

The people forgot People-Builder for eighteen summers of oppression. Then they began to look once more beyond the sky. They remembered that he is always close and always cares. Families throughout the central highlands began to travel to the Place of Peace. Once more they sacrificed spotless newborn lambs to People-Builder. They asked forgiveness and renewed their commitment. They called for help. Smoke and sincere requests drifted upward.

The one who is above all turned toward the New Land. His voice was carried on the wind to a lonely hill where a young man tended sheep.

"My people call for help and I choose you to be my instrument. If you follow me, you will be a great warrior and honored by all who have shunned you."

"Honor means nothing to me," Left Hand answered. "I simply want to be alone with my sheep. But first I will do whatever you ask."

"Follow and I will show you how to defeat your enemy."

Left Hand purchased heavy bronze and in his father's forge made for himself a thick two-edged dagger. He sharpened it and practiced handling it until he could slice through a rope with a single stroke. He sewed strips of leather into a sheath that could be strapped to the inside of his right thigh and was unnoticeable beneath his robe.

When it was time to pay tribute, he went to the grand palace in the rebuilt city and stood before the round king.

"I have brought you half my father's newborn lambs," said Left Hand. "I also have a private message that will be of great importance to you. But it should not be spoken in public. My life will end if my people learn what I have told you. I must meet with you in secrecy."

The king had lived well and long because he was not easily deceived.

Assassins had tried to kill him and had failed. They had died very slowly at his hand.

But before him stood a small shepherd.

He saw no weapon or threat.

Guards felt his robes and found nothing.

"Leave us alone," he ordered, dismissing all his guards and servants. They left the hall and closed the great curtains at its entrance.

The king stood and approached the shepherd. "Now, what is this message?" the king demanded. "And who is it from?"

"The message I have to give you is from the one who lives beyond the sky and holds the stars in his hands."

The shepherd spoke softly, so the king stepped closer. So did the strange little shepherd. They were within arm's reach of one another. The young warrior held out his right hand to grasp the king's arm in greeting.

The left slipped beneath his robe.

"This is what People-Builder declares," said Left Hand. "I will allow the oppression of my people no longer."

From nowhere the bright dagger flashed. It sliced through the fine clothes of the king. It slipped downward into the king's large body with a powerful thrust. So deep did Left Hand drive the blade that even the handle disappeared inside his flesh.

He could have yelled out, but the king was simply too surprised. This would be his assassin? The round one stood silent, mouth open and eyes fixed in disbelief. He grabbed at his stomach as his royal robe absorbed his blood and turned ever more crimson.

"Oh king," said Left Hand, "your message from People-Builder is that anyone who harms my children will have to face their protector. You rebuilt the mighty city and yet you shall fall, just as its tall walls and thick gates crumbled during the days of Point Man. No one can stand in defiance of the one who is above all things."

The king remained standing in eerie silence. He turned his back on Left Hand and tried to find a place to sit. Almost in slow motion he staggered, step by step through the doorway into his private chamber. His movements must have thrown weight against the door, for it slammed and the fine lock fell into place.

Left Hand stood alone in the grand throne room. He could hardly believe that no alarm had been sounded. A piece of purple dyed linen lay before him on the great chair the round king had occupied in splendor a few minutes before.

He picked it up and wiped the blood from his hand and forearm. He repositioned the cloth on the chair and turned and walked calmly from the hall.

Outside servants and soldiers were milling about to look busy.

"Your lord has gone into his chamber," he remarked as he passed. "He will call when he is ready for you."

With that he walked out the front door, passing more well-armed guards who waited for the king to order their return. The servants and guards waited until long after Left Hand had departed before daring to knock and then call at the chamber door. When there was no answer, they finally burst through the heavy curtains that enclosed the room. All was dark. Perhaps their king did sleep still.

But no. Dimly the light from a small shuttered window revealed the great bulk of a man who lay face down in the middle of the room. A guard rolled the king onto his back and checked for life. But the breath was still and the heart quiet.

"Stop him!" yelled the head guard. "Don't let Left Hand leave the city. Close the gates."

By that time the young warrior had already slipped through the gates and was heading into the hills beyond. On the highest hill, a hill not far from a few villages, he held a great ram's horn to his lips. The long, mournful wail of the ancient battle cry sounded again and again as he turned to face each direction. In the distance other rams' horns could now be heard. Throughout the highlands men heard the call and put down their seed bags and unyoked their oxen. They put on leather coverings and grabbed sharp swords. As the sun faded, many men were walking to answer the horn blast. As light returned, several hundred of all ages stood before Left Hand. A few may have remembered that they had once ridiculed the boy of the left hand. None were laughing now as Left Hand shouted words they had thought they would never hear:

"People-Builder is our victory!

"People-Builder is our sword and shield!

"This day People-Builder will free us from our enemy!"

The warriors cheered and marched toward the city. The city itself was in turmoil, for word had spread of the death of the king. Commanding officers tried to take control, but they had no real authority without the king, and few would listen to them. The streets were full of chaos and crowds and confusion.

When the warriors could be seen approaching, panic froze the assembling defenders, and they put up little more than token resistance. A mob of citizens ran for the river. But the warriors of Left Hand were already there, barring the way.

The head of the city guard finally rallied the demoralized army.

"See, there, that man in front. He killed our king with his own hand. Are we going to surrender? Or will we revenge our king with the deaths of his murderers? We are far more than they."

Finally he pulled together the army—thousands of valiant men with sharp swords. They charged toward the bank of the Winding River. They charged toward the army of People-Builder that was gathered there.

But in the end, it was their blood that trickled into the water. Their bodies floated off with the current.

The invaders ruled no longer.

The land was free.

People-Builder was their victory.

And each soldier in the army of People-Builder held up his sword—each clutched in the left hand—and cheered. Never again would a left-handed man be ashamed to walk in the land of People-Builder.

Around great fires along the river the victors enjoyed food and friendship, wine and laughter, stories and music. They gave gratitude to the one who is above all. Early the next morning, Left Hand walked with People-Builder. He walked west past the deserted city and into the hills where he had shepherded his father's flocks. He found a shepherd there and purchased a spotless lamb. He carried it across his shoulders as he set off toward the Place of Peace.

"I will return to make my sacrifice," he told the keepers of the Special Place as he left the lamb in their keeping. North he walked, to the highlands, to the tall monument standing white as sparkling snow against the blue sky. This monument stood in remembrance of the vow made by the people in the days of Point Man.

"I will follow the ways of People-Builder with all my heart and with all my soul," he declared before the dazzling monument.

A light sprinkle dampened his face. A rainbow arched across the highlands. The ancient stories came back to him:

"Yes, I will always remember," he told the one who is above all. "I will remember that you are always close and will always care."

Left Hand remembered the moment of the rainbow always. During his days the new land had rest, and the People of the Promise kept their eyes on the one who lives beyond the sky and holds the stars in his hands.

THE SMALLEST DETAILS CAN DESTROY
THE GREATEST FORCES.

CHAPTER 4

BEEKEEPER'S WIFE

Left Hand kept peace among the People of the Promise. He resolved conflicts and answered questions and settled disagreements. His life was faultless so all respected his words and listened to his decisions. Wisdom ruled until Left Hand grew old.

His eyesight grew dark.

His ears were dimmed.

His energy turned to exhaustion.

Someone would have to come after him to lead the People of the Promise. At last he heard of one who possessed strength and heart, who had wisdom and discernment and commanded respect. Each morning this person walked with People-Builder near the Place of the Portal and had once even dreamed of a silver staircase with hundreds of glowing angels traveling its steps.

As Left Hand grew enfeebled, it was Beekeeper's Wife who led in his place.

Left Hand had not convinced many to walk in the ways of People-Builder. Long before he passed from the blue planet the people forgot past victories and walked paths of their own fashioning. Those paths inevitably led deeper into chaos. In dark and murky corners the New Land became a place of anarchy.

When Beekeeper's Wife called the people to the Place of Peace, they ignored her. When she encouraged them to place the cut of commitment upon their children, they turned away. When she begged them to cry to the one above all things, some even laughed.

But when the People of the Hills began to take away the lands, they listened.

North of the stormy sea the people left the forests and rebuilt the

163

Double City. They claimed it as their capital and crowned a grandson of the proud king who had gathered the fourteen cities against Point Man. Their most courageous warrior was called to be captain of a new army. They made alliances with those who forged metal. Soon the army had nine hundred chariots of iron. They pointed their chariots and horsemen and footmen southward, and none stood before them. For twenty summers they ruled the land and enslaved the people and crushed anyone who threatened their tight-fisted control.

But Beekeeper's Wife walked each day with People-Builder. She wandered the countryside calling the people to look to the highlands. She patiently called them to make People-Builder their sword and shield against chariots of iron.

Now they asked her advice. They followed her wise council. They returned to the Place of Peace and looked to the highlands and cried out to the one above all things. People-Builder looked down on these broken slaves. Sorrow filled his eyes as it had when he had seen his people enslaved in the Land of the Pyramids.

Wind rustled the palms surrounding the house of Beekeeper's Wife. Long she had sought its whisper. But she did not expect what it said.

"Since the conquering of the land, I have asked two leaders to take up swords to free my people," said the wind.

"I chose Lion.

"I chose Left Hand.

"Now I choose you."

"Oh People-Builder, I long to hear your words across the land. Give me wisdom to choose a commander for our army."

"No. I know many young men of courage. I do not go to one of them to free the people. I choose you."

She lifted her head to look beyond the sky.

"I have been a mother to the People of the Promise. Now I am a grandmother to them. You gave me gentle hands and unwearied feet to take your message, but you did not give me strength to lift a sword. I cannot free your people."

"Do you refuse to go?"

"I will go anywhere, but I am no warrior."

"You need not be a warrior," said the wind. "I will send you north of the Double City to one who can lead my army onto the field."

Beekeeper's Wife was uncertain but hopeful as she sent messengers north beyond the Double City to search out a man known as Lightning. She walked continually with People-Builder to seek the way.

Lightning met Beekeeper's Wife beneath the palm trees where she advised the people.

"Will you lead the army?" she asked.

"I see no army," said Lightning.

"People-Builder will provide an army."

"I see no weapons."

"People-Builder will provide means and a plan."

"Then I will do my part," said Lightning. "Together we will lead the people into battle. I will be your warrior."

"My place is to lead the people toward People-Builder. It is your place to stand on the battlefield."

"You have walked many years with People-Builder and know his voice. You must go with me into battle to tell me his words."

The eyes of the old woman flashed as she looked over her nervous warrior: "Has this people wandered so far that none hears his voice or steps out in confidence? Yes, I will go with you into battle. But know this, Lightning. It will always be said that this battle was won by women."

"Come to the hill country. Bring your weapons."

Runners took the call throughout the villages. Beekeeper's Wife and Lightning journeyed three days to the hill country beyond the Double City. Fearful but tired of the harsh rulers, men sharpened their fathers' swords on millstones. They quickly worked fat into raw leather and made new fastenings for old armor, much of it stripped off enemy bodies on long ago battlefields.

Slowly and steadily and secretly, ten thousand men gathered from the northern tribes. Quickly their weapons were tested and repaired. Wooden shields were covered with leather. Farmers were trained in the basics of war. These soldiers had great desire but no time. Already they had to stay on the move as they trained. A superior force searched for them.

Finally they picked their battlefield and led their army to the slopes of Round-Topped Mountain.

The captain of the chariots moved his army down the dry bed of the

Western River at the base of Round-Topped Mountain. It was a frightening force that sent dust high into the afternoon air and turned the sun red. Beekeeper's Wife watched the chariots approach. She could only imagine what damage those chariots could do. But even though the opposing army was larger and more powerful, People-Builder had promised victory. She wondered what amazing thing she was about to see.

Far to the east at the enemy's back, a dark storm cloud threatened. It became thick and dangerous and more angry looking. The eyes of Beekeeper's Wife moved past the dust of the chariots. She closely watched the cloud poised at the horizon and a plan was passed along the line.

"When the storm strikes the upper valley," whispered People-Builder, "charge the chariots."

Suddenly the storm cloud moved in and broke open with fury. The downpour soaked the dusty ground and collected in the dry streambeds of the hills. Springs and rivulets and cascades rushed to feed the river.

Horses reared and broke ranks and stampeded in confusion.

Iron wheels sank in mud.

Lightning blew his ram's horn.

Now a flood of men joined the waters, hurling down the hillside swinging swords and shouldering shields. The commanders of the hill people took charge and formed their ranks. The chariots that still moved finally were turned toward the attackers and prepared for battle. The enemy was confident that even a reduced force could destroy this ill-clad mob.

But things had started badly. Chariots had speed, but the flood and storm so confused the forces that the charioteers did not have a clear idea which way to strike. Their hesitation was fatal as Lightning's warriors overwhelmed the scattered horsemen and charioteers and foot soldiers. The People of the Promise were strong and courageous. Metal struck metal. Horses fell. Chariots were useless. Both sides held their ground until a second ram's horn was heard on the hilltop. Almost as quickly as they had come the warriors of Lightning retreated up the steep hillsides.

What Beekeeper's Wife alone could see on her hilltop was the dam of floating debris that had collected at a narrow bottleneck in the waterway. An immense lake of water had collected behind the natural dam.

The enemy did nothing for long moments, surprised that the attack had been broken off. They were so confused that they regrouped at the river's edge before following the fleeing warriors.

That was where they were when the dam broke and a thundering wall of water crashed down the valley. They saw the flood approach and fear tightened each weathered face. There was only one direction to go—along the river bed—so the captain screamed at his men to outrun the mighty flow. Terrified horses hardly felt the whips as they galloped with foam and fury. There was never much of a race.

The waters raged.

The horse hooves thundered.

The seasoned soldiers screamed.

By ones and twos and threes chariots were swallowed. The captain leaped to the riverbank just as his invincible iron machine disappeared. Many foot soldiers climbed free of the flood, but now they were trapped between waters of death and swords of death. The warriors of People-Builder charged back down the mountainside to claim the survivors. Somehow the captain fought his way through with reckless valor and ran on foot north toward the security of the Double City.

The captain ran for hours, hiding then running then hiding.

He was exhausted and defeated and desperate.

He pushed himself as is possible only when death nips at the heels.

The sun set. He was halfway to the Double City when he saw the fire lights of a small camp of metalworkers who served the king. At last he could relax and find shelter.

A care-worn woman saw the captain stagger toward the fires. She recognized him and remembered his pride and cruelty to her people. But she went up to him with a smile of welcome.

"You seem harried by an enemy. Come my captain. You can rest safe here."

"Thank you," he panted and slowly dragged the final steps to her tent. She gave him milk and a blanket.

"Someone may follow, seeking my life," he murmured as he lay on the pallet. "Stand and watch. You will be rewarded," said the captain with the last of his energy. "If anyone approaches, awaken me."

He collapsed into a deep sleep. He did not feel the prick of the sharpened tent peg placed on his temple. He did not see the wooden hammer lifted high to strike the tent peg. After that, he felt nothing ever again.

Silently she watched the captain's life soak into the sleeping mat.

When soldiers of the People of the Promise came through the camp at daylight, the woman showed them the empty body beneath her blanket.

Lightning bowed deeply before her with a laugh. "You have taken away any glory that would have been mine this day," he said. "You have done what no man was able to. Our oppression is over."

That night, warriors gathered to hear a song of celebration—

It was a song of two women—

two women used by the one who is infinite and eternal and all powerful—

two women who defeated an army of chariots.

CHAPTER 5

MIGHTY WARRIOR

Tall, dark men with sharp curved swords swept westward. They covered ground quickly on their large loping camels. Nomads, they lived well off the labors of others. Golden crescents dangled from their ears. Their fingers sparkled with heavy jeweled rings. Like swarms of locusts, they came at harvesttime, raiding and pillaging. They left dead those who resisted giving their crops. They left starving those who submitted. Their animals ate what they did not steal and trampled the rest.

The People of the Promise organized. They fought valiantly. But the raiders came in forces too great to drive off. Battle seemed hopeless, so they took their crops at harvesttime and hid.

Some fled to the forests.

Some hid in the hills.

Others disappeared into hidden camps and caves and highland clefts.

For seven summers the desert people ravaged the land, sucking all the life from the ground and leaving nothing but famine. Finally the people went to the Place of Peace and cried to People-Builder for help.

The chief keeper of the Special Place stood before a ragged crowd and asked, "Why should the one above all answer your cry? You have forgotten his words and abandoned his ways. You follow the paths of Shining One. You are no different than the people of the hills or the people of the plains or the people of the desert.

"People-Builder will help you," continued the chief keeper, "for he will not turn his back on anyone with a sincere heart and a desperate need. Turn now to him and he will give you a mighty warrior who will free you from your enemy."

A cycle of the moon passed and it was the dangerous time of harvest. In the southern shadow of Round-Top mountain, a farmer threshed his grain at twilight beneath rock outcroppings on a hillside. His eyes scanned the horizon nervously as he worked hard and fast, hoping to go unseen by the enemy. Fifteen summers before he had been a soldier in Lightning's army. He had shown great courage on that day. But things were different now and he was afraid. Everyone was afraid. Oh, for such a leader as Lightning.

Suddenly a man twice as tall as he stood at his side. His right hand held an ancient shepherd's staff. His face glowed and his eyes sparkled and his mouth spoke with gentle words that calmed a fear-filled heart.

"People-Builder is with you and he will make you a mighty warrior once more."

The farmer nearly collapsed from fright for he had not heard the approach nor ever seen such a glowing figure as now spoke to him:

"The one beyond the sky has not forgotten. He is calling you to free his people from their enemy."

The man knew he must be having a vivid dream—or else a visitation such as happened in days of old. He sank to his knees and looked up at the magnificent creature before him. He felt the need to fall prostrate before such a one, but somehow he knew that this would not be right. So he held out his hands to the angel.

"Look at me," said the man. "See the large and stained and clumsy hands of a farmer. How can I free anybody? I am too timid to stand up for myself, let alone my people."

"People-Builder will be your sword and your shield and your strength."

"Stay. Tell me more," said the man. "Let me prepare you a meal and you can explain to me how this can be possible."

"I will stay," said the angel.

More afraid of this visitor than any approaching marauders, the farmer lit an evening fire and warmed his lamb stew. He set out the meat and bread on a large rock beneath a spreading oak. The angel touched the food with the tip of his shepherd's staff. A burst of fire flared from the rock and then was gone. So were the meat and bread. The man stared in shock and surprise. This was no dream, he decided, for his dreaming mind could never invent such a story as he was living. He remembered the words of Lightning before they had driven out their enemy: "Impossibilities never limit People-Builder."

"Tell me what to do."

"First purge your village of its evil. Destroy the altar to Shining One and cut down the pole with the carvings of snakes. Then bring the stones and wood to this hillside. Build an altar to the one who holds stars in his hands and use the pole to start a fire and sacrifice a bull as a token of your commitment."

Late that night when all was quiet, ten men tore down the altar. They carried off the stones in a donkey cart. The town people awoke to discover that their altar was missing and its foundation stones dug up. Their pole of snakes had been chopped off at its base.

"How could this have happened?" they cried. "Shining One will be furious."

"Look!" Eyes squinted in the morning sun and focused on the hillside above the small city where smoke curled upward from a burning sacrifice on a new altar. When they reached the altar, they saw that it had been built of their old stones. Now its burnt offering was to People-Builder.

"Who would have done such a thing?" they asked each other.

The frightened wife of one of the ten men gave a name. "Anyone who defies Shining One must die!" shouted angry voices as the crowd surged toward the house of the mighty warrior's father.

"Give us your son!" they demanded. "He has disgraced Shining One and we must stone him."

"Can't the serpent take care of himself?" asked the father. "If Shining One is really so powerful, let him destroy my son. But if the snake is mere arrogance and emptiness, my son has done us all a favor."

That made sense. They listened and agreed and returned to their homes, watching to see what would happen to the altar breaker. When he finished his harvest openly and unafraid and unthreatened by raiders, his point was made.

A cycle of the moon later, the mighty warrior sent messengers to the northern tribes calling all able-bodied men to gather at the Rippling Spring.

The mighty warrior looked beyond the sky, "Are you sure you want me for this great task?"

There was silence.

"I will place a wool fleece on the ground overnight," said the warrior. "If in the morning the fleece is damp with dew and the ground is dry, I will know you want me to free my people."

The next morning the fleece was damp with dew and the ground was dry. But he still wondered. "I will place the same wool fleece on the ground overnight," he said. "This time if the fleece is dry and the ground is damp with dew, I will know you want me to free my people."

The next morning the fleece was dry and the ground was damp with dew. The farmer could no longer question his calling. He was no longer a farmer but Mighty Warrior.

In a few days, he stood at the Rippling Spring. It was not a huge army but with People-Builder perhaps they could do it.

"You have too many warriors at the spring. Send some of them home."

"We need many more than this to fight well-armed raiders on camels."

"Am I not more than warriors on camels?"

The warrior called his army together. "We look to People-Builder for our victory, not might of arms. Many of you have a fear-filled heart. All is well. Go home without disgrace, but watch to see what People-Builder will do."

Through the day, men wandered from the camp and did not return. Still a multitude of ten thousand stood before Mighty Warrior. It was still too many.

"All of you, go to the edge of the spring to drink a few at a time. Mighty Warrior pulled aside all who drank recklessly and carelessly and without watching the surroundings. These he thanked and bid return home.

Three hundred men remained.

"With these men you shall free your people from their enemy," said the wind. "Though the invaders are as thick as locusts and as numerous as the sands on the seashore they shall fall this night."

As darkness filled the land, the small army was divided into three equal companies. Each man was equipped with:

A ram's horn hung from one shoulder;

A torch was in one hand and a pottery vase in the other;

A sharp sword was strapped to each back.

The raiders had returned to take the second harvest of grain and they all camped together in a great mass of men and camels. They chose a valley surrounded by high hills. It was not a good place to defend, but who would bother them?

Shortly before midnight, the three hundred marched an hour north across a wide valley and silently surrounded the camp of the desert people.

They were deep in sleep and their guards were even nodding off as the three companies crept into place.

Suddenly the night was split by the wail of a ram's horn. A moment later, three hundred rams' horns rattled the tents of the desert warriors. Men stumbled groggily from their tents.

Then each of the three hundred shattered the vase that had covered their torch. The surrounding hills looked ablaze.

Mighty Warrior's men gave a thunderous battle cry and waved their torches. Camels stampeded and tents collapsed and panicking desert people ran to and fro. Again the rams' horns blew, closer this time. It was very dark in the camp, but in the hills it was bright. If each torch was a company, the enemy soldiers must be all around. Swords flashed in all directions. Weapons were raised to strike down all threats. Without knowing friend from foe, the raiders slashed down their comrades. Survivors fled toward the Winding River and their homeland. It was a stampede of men and women and children. With them ran camels and cattle and sheep.

Mighty Warrior sent messengers to gather all who had been sent home. Enough of these men were still about to cut off the raiders by blocking the fords of the Winding River. Women and children were allowed to pass. Cattle and sheep were calmed and gathered in nearby fields. The men with golden crescents appeared in small frightened groups at the fords, many unarmed. These were all killed. A great quantity of gold earrings and jeweled rings was collected.

The People of the Promise divided the spoils of grain and food and animals. None would go hungry this year.

Families crept from the forests.

Shepherds drove sheep from hiding places in the hills.

They left the camps and caves and clefts.

"With just a handful of men you defeated an enemy as vast as the sand on the seashore!" cried the people as they mobbed Mighty Warrior.

"With People-Builder even the impossible can take place," said the warrior as he walked toward his farm.

CHAPTER 6

RENEGADE

Peace rested on the land, but a tainted peace. Enemies did not invade and yet uneasiness taunted the hearts of all who did not fix their gaze beyond the sky. The People of the Promise said they listened to People-Builder's words, but they did not really know his voice. They insisted they walked his ways, but when their paths diverged from his nobody really knew they had gone astray.

Mighty Warrior also wandered. He married many women and had many sons. He ignored those things he had once honored. He walked ways that saddened the one above all. He abandoned his wives and neglected his children. One son in particular missed his father's notice and direction. As this boy grew, Shining One whispered in his ear. The ancient snake raised this boy as his own, training him thoroughly in the passions of pride and the arts of anarchy. The serpent named him Renegade. He was bitter toward his father and resented his brothers and ridiculed People-Builder.

"Someday I will rule this land.

"Someday people will bow to me.

"Someday I will be mightier than the Mighty Warrior."

Seventy sons met at their father's home in the southern shadow of Round-Top Mountain. There Mighty Warrior breathed his last. The sons carried their father to a nearby cave and laid him next to his father.

A snake waited at its entrance.

"Who will take your father's place?" hissed Shining One. "There are many of you but room for only one leader."

"Such decisions will wait; today we drop our eyes and mourn our father."

Two days south, Renegade didn't have time to mourn. He went to his uncles at the City of Oaks and asked for silver. The city was a place of anarchy where his wealthy uncles sat beneath a grove of spreading trees. Those trees were descended from the great oak where Wrestler had buried the bag of evil charms so long ago. Perhaps a little of that evil remained in the ground and trees.

"Why should we give you silver?" asked his uncles.

"I will turn silver into power," said Renegade. "I will rule the New Land. I will make the City of Oaks its capital and you will have more wealth than your storehouses can hold."

"But what about the other sons?"

"Give me silver. Then we shall see who rules."

His uncles gave him silver from the temple of Shining One. Renegade went to the crossroads to hire men to fight for him. Then with a serpent's heart, he traveled north to visit his half-brothers.

"Now is the time I've trained you for," said the snake. "Spill blood and take your crown."

"Brothers," he said, "I am sorry for my hatred toward our father. I join you to mourn him. Let us gather at the rock where he met the angel and weep together."

His brothers embraced Renegade and tears fell freely. When the warriors rushed from hiding, the massacre took only moments. Sixty-nine bodies lay lifeless at the large stone. Blood colored the rock where the angel had consumed food with fire. Blood flowed onto the ground where Mighty Warrior had knelt.

The snake laughed.

The paid warriors hailed Renegade.

Inside the house the youngest son crouched.

He had seen it all, frozen in disbelief. Now he had to flee, for once they realized someone was missing, they would hunt him down. Out the door and down the hill he sprinted without looking back. He ran until he fell exhausted in a bed of the softest grass and slept.

As night drew near, he crawled into a secluded cave and cried, "People-Builder, help me. What shall I do?"

A gentle breeze blew through the darkness. "I will be your shelter. Rest in me and I will show you the way."

Calm soothed his troubled heart. His eyes closed. He faded into a peaceful dreamless sleep.

A week passed, and the youngest son remained hidden in the darkness of the cave except for night forages for food and water. Then the wind blew again. "It is time to follow me," whistled its voice.

So the youngest followed People-Builder to a mountain ledge overlooking the City of Oaks. He watched the sun lift above the Mountains of the Dawn and waited.

It was the day of Renegade's parade of triumph. A large crowd gathered near the oaks and cheered his return. They admired his ruthlessness and thought him an ideal king. His uncles had commissioned a golden crown and a royal robe. Renegade reveled in their adoration, while Shining One gloated at the town's celebration of violence and anarchy.

As the golden crown was about to be placed on Renegade's head, a voice of considerable power interrupted the coronation. All stopped and looked around. Was Renegade the source? He looked as confused as anyone. As the voice continued, someone decided that it was coming from the direction of the mountain. They could barely see the man on the mountain ledge that overlooked the city. Yet his voice continued, strong and clear and unearthly.

"I have come from People-Builder.

"He has sent you a story in honor of this great event."

The crowd stood silent.

"There once was a meeting of trees. They decided the forest would be a much better place if only it had a ruler. So they agreed to ask the olive tree.

"The olive tree shook its leafy head. 'No, I do not want to be king, for the one above all has given me a great task. I produce a special fruit with golden oil that makes people glad.'

"So they went to the fig tree and asked if he would rule over them.

"The fig tree rustled a polite refusal. 'The one above all has already given me a great task. I produce a prosperous fruit that nourishes the body and has a sweet taste that makes people glad.'

"So they went to the grapevine and asked.

" 'The one above all has already given me a great task. I produce a cheerful fruit with sparkling juice that makes people glad,' replied the grapevine.

"In desperation the trees turned to the bramble: 'Will you be our king?'

" The bramble readily agreed. 'The one above all has not given me a job. I produce nothing of value. But you must do all that I wish or I will have you cut down.'

"People-Builder asks that you consider carefully your choice of king!" shouted the youngest brother. "If you choose a person of honor, life will be full of peace. If you choose a person of anarchy, life will be full of destruction."

"Kill him!" screamed Renegade.

By the time the paid fighters had raced up the mountain, the brother had long disappeared and hidden himself deep in his secret cave. They found no trace of the one who shouted from the mountain. At the City of Oaks the joyful mood was dampened, but they still placed a gold crown on Renegade's head and set a royal robe around his shoulders.

Music played.

And people danced.

And the serpent sunned itself at the city gate.

Three summers passed and the people of the city grew restless. They came to see the wicked heart of Renegade. They felt shame for their part in the murders of Mighty Warrior's sons. Wealth had come to the city, but much of it ended up in Renegade's storehouses and benefited no one but him.

So when Renegade left the city to survey his land, the uncles plotted. It was the time of harvest and crowds filled the fields where they ate and drank and cursed Renegade.

"When he returns," they cried, "let us set up an ambush. We will treat him as he did his brothers."

The governor of the city secretly sent a messenger to warn Renegade that the people had turned against him. "When you return, bring more paid fighters. Come in the dark of night and hide in the fields until the sun lights the sky. Be prepared for ambush and act quickly."

Renegade heeded the governor's warning: He came in the dark of night and hid in the fields until the sun lit the sky. When the people saw that their king was outside the city, they rushed to attack. His mercenaries struck from their hiding places with reckless vengeance. The city people were farmers, not soldiers. They fought, and many fell in their fields. As dusk dimmed their vision, those who remained retreated to the city and barred the heavy wooden gates.

When light returned, the people of the city looked from their walls and saw no one. Renegade and his fighters were gone.

The men of the city cautiously opened the gates. They came out to look around and nothing happened. So they went out to the fields to finish their harvest.

A cry tore the quiet. Soldiers jumped up from the ground and burst from the brambles. The city people tried to defend themselves, but harvesting hooks were no match for weapons. Survivors raced for the gates, but more soldiers cut them off. Within moments all lay motionless, and the mercenaries hurried toward the city.

The paid fighters smashed again and again at the gate with a large log. It was not a strong gate, and Renegade led the assault and demolished the city and killed its people.

"We have destroyed the city that turned against me," said Renegade. "But another city has sided with my brother. Let us do there what we have done here."

The second city was smaller than the first, and its gate fell quickly. But these people flocked to a large tower and crowded in.

The doors would not budge. So his men circled the stronghold with wood and prepared to burn it. But none looked up.

High above, on the top of the tower, a woman waited and watched. A heavy stone had been set on the edge.

As Renegade ordered his troops to pile wood high, he came closer and closer to the spot under where the woman waited. She had one chance. If she failed, they would all die. For a moment he stood in the right place and then moved. Then he was back. With no hesitation but a breathed word to People-Builder, the woman pushed and the stone dropped. Renegade was struck and dropped without a sound.

He groaned and coughed and slowly regained a dazed consciousness.

"Help me," he begged in a weak voice to the soldier who cradled his head and gave him water.

"I'm sorry," he said, "I can do nothing more."

"It can't end this way," gasped Renegade. "Where is Shining One? Can't he save me? I was to rule. They were to bow to me. I would be mightier than Mighty Warrior."

"Lie quietly," said the soldier.

"Was it a great warrior who caused my death?"

"A woman. She dropped a stone."

"Then kill me," ordered Renegade. "Run your sword through my heart so none can say that the mightiest was killed by a woman."

The mercenary gently laid his commander down. He pulled his sword and made a quick upward thrust.

The fighters slowly turned away from the tower and walked out through the ruined city. Renegade would be remembered, not as a mighty warrior, but as a bramble pulled up by a woman. His name became a byword of disgrace throughout the land. His body lay unclaimed where it was dumped outside the city wall.

The People of the Promise looked beyond the sky and they remembered the words of the youngest brother. "If you choose a man of anarchy, life will be full of destruction." Those who had crowned Renegade had been destroyed by him and his capital city no longer existed.

So the people of the New Land turned toward People-Builder and journeyed to the Place of Peace and sacrificed spotless newborn lambs. As the smoke lifted, so did their voices.

"You are our sword and shield.

"You are our shelter.

"You are our king."

NOT ALL THE TOMORROWS
CAN TAKE BACK
A SINGLE MOMENT
OF YESTERDAY.

CHAPTER 7

OUTCAST

Strong leaders ruled the New Land and called all to the Place of Peace. But these leaders grew old and died, and after each generation the chaos in the land seemed worse than ever before. Men who did not know the ways of People-Builder strived for power. Tribes lost their unity and argued and battled each other. Lives were lost or ruined.

The root of trouble was always the same: It was easier to offer sacrifices to the images of Shining One than to look beyond the sky to one who is infinite and eternal and all-powerful. And once the people turned toward Shining One it was ever so hard to turn away. So the one above all removed his sword and shield and strength from the New Land. He stepped aside.

Another king of the plain sent yet another army. This time they invaded the Plains of Comfort, shattering cities and crushing people of the tribes that had settled east of the Winding River. They declared themselves invincible conquerors. For eighteen summers they ruled the tribes and none from west of the river crossed to oppose them. So plains warriors crossed the Winding River to conquer the rest of the New Land.

The people of the west bank panicked. A thousand spotless newborn lambs were sacrificed to the silent statues, but the statues remained silent. A thousand bonfires were built and people cut themselves as they cried out to Shining One, but the armies did not stop. Cruel soldiers burned land and toppled buildings and carried children away to be slaves.

In sadness and despair the people looked to the highlands. "Please hear our pain and help us."

"I am listening," whispered the wind.

"We have hurt you. When you spoke, we refused to hear. When you led, we refused to follow. Now we see our foolishness."

"You have many statues of Shining One. Go plead your case."

"We were deceived," said the people. "The statues are worthless; Shining One lies."

"Words come easy for you. What will you do?"

Within three days every statue of Shining One had been shattered. The pieces were broken down or melted down or ground into dust. The tribes humbled their hearts and lifted their voices beyond the sky.

As the people cried to the one above all, billowy clouds of purest white drifted overhead. A soft rain splashed away their tears and stretched a colorful arch across the sky.

"This is your answer and your reminder," said a keeper of the Special Place. "A reminder that People-Builder keeps his promises. He is always close, and he will always care."

Hope bloomed. If People-Builder was with them, the invaders would soon be gone. But they wondered where and when and how the deliverance would come.

As a large company of enemy soldiers gathered at the watchtower on the eastern borderlands, two watchers crept through the shadows to listen to their drunken talk.

How easy to conquer this land of milk and honey, they boasted.

How weak and fearful and foolish these people were.

How they would drive these people from the Winding River.

Soon the land would belong to the Plains People once again, and this time it would be theirs forever.

The watchers reported all.

"It is time to reclaim our land," said the elders. "Anyone who will take us into battle against these invaders will be our leader for the rest of his days."

No one stepped forward.

"Only one warrior in the land has the experience and courage to do this work," said one man at last. "He is my half-brother—our father's child by a foreign woman. Their son was named Outcast, for he was driven away and has no home. He leads ruffians who fight for anyone who pays them."

"I know these men," said another. "They have already been harassing the People of the Plains, stealing and skirmishing and setting their tents on fire."

A delegation of elders went to Outcast.

"Why should I lead a people who has driven me from the town of my father?" demanded Outcast.

"All will welcome you once you drive out the People of the Plains."

"You will be our respected one and our warrior and our ruler."

"Why should I believe you?" asked Outcast. "You follow the ways of Shining One."

"We have shattered and burned and ground to dust our statues. We have made our vows to People-Builder."

"You have made your vows? I wonder how well you will keep them. I will never let one of my vows to People-Builder go unfulfilled. Yes, I will be your warrior and lead your army. Then I, the outcast, will be your ruler and see that you keep these promises."

A messenger approached the camp of the king of the plains.

"You bring a final surrender?" asked the king.

"I bring words from Outcast who speaks for People-Builder: 'Why have you invaded the New Land? You must withdraw immediately or be destroyed.' "

The king could not believe a defeated people would send such a brazen message: "Tell Outcast that this land is ours. When you came from the Land of Pyramids, Point Man took it. Now it will be returned. Lay down your swords before us. Perhaps we will let you live as our servants."

Outcast sent the messenger back with his reply: "People-Builder, who made the blue planet and all its lands, gave us this land. We have cultivated it for three hundred summers. You are not fighting against us but against the one who lives beyond the sky and holds stars in his hands. If you are a wise king who loves your people, you will quietly leave before harvest whitens the fields."

"Who does this Outcast think he is?" shouted the king. He was so enraged that he pulled his sword and ran it through the messenger. "We will attack this army without mercy. The head of Outcast will hang from the watchtower for all to see."

When Outcast heard this, he looked beyond the sky. "Hear these threats. They are not against me but against your honor."

The wind blew strong and whispered, "I am your victory."

So excited was Outcast in the passion of the moment that he did not notice the wind. He lifted his hands to the sky:

"Hear me, People-Builder.

"Hear me and I will give wondrous sacrifices.

"Hear me and I will sacrifice whatever I first see when I return to my lands."

And the wind grew suddenly still.

Outcast lifted his sword, and his army followed. They fought fiercely and valiantly and left the invading soldiers strewn across the field. Those who could, fled without shame. In the end only a small knot of soldiers stood in the shadow of the eastern watchtower and would not retreat. In their center stood the king with courage and arrogance.

The king and Outcast faced each other in the dying light of day.

"Where is your army?" asked Outcast.

"I need no army to deal with outcasts and children of slaves," blustered the king. "I have Shining One and need nothing else."

"You have followed him faithfully, but you must see that Shining One is powerless before People-Builder or our army would never have stood before yours."

"Raise your weapon and let us see who gives the greatest strength."

The two fought until their arms could hardly lift sword and shield. The land was turning dark, yet neither would give way. Outcast was younger but the king more experienced. Finally Outcast seemed to drop his guard. The king saw the opening and lunged as his opponent stepped aside and caught him on the point of his sword. The king lay with the same wound he had given the messenger.

During the next cycle of the moon the army removed every invader from the New Land. The victory was glorious and the people declared Outcast their most respected leader and warrior and ruler. A grand procession of elders returned him to his home in triumph.

Outcast's wife and beautiful ten-year-old daughter were so proud of him. His wife prepared a great feast. His daughter practiced a celebration dance. Both waited with loving anticipation for the sound of his footsteps.

As Outcast reached his land, his daughter ran to meet him with a tambourine and a giggle. She reached the men and began a whirling dance of grace and joy.

But the father and elders looked on in horror.

The dance ended and the girl saw their faces and was hurt. She ran to her father.

"Why do you look so sad? Did you not like my dance? You seem ready to cry."

Outcast embraced his daughter tightly. "I love your dance and I love you, but you have broken me upon my own rash words."

The wife of Outcast now reached the group and the elders gathered around.

"None expect you to keep such a vow."

"Give a newborn lamb instead."

"Certainly People-Builder will understand."

His wife heard snatches of what was said and interrupted: "My husband is a man of honor. If he has made a vow, he will keep it no matter how difficult."

But she soon turned silent in horror with her daughter as she understood.

"My vow was foolish and I don't know what to do," said Outcast as he placed his right arm around his wife and his left arm around his daughter. "I said if People-Builder gave me victory I would sacrifice on a stone altar the first thing that came to me as I returned to my lands."

His wife broke into sobs and his daughter stood in shock.

"It is only a vow to People-Builder. We will release you from it," insisted the elders.

"Yes, only to People-Builder," repeated Outcast. "Is that why our people turn to Shining One? They have no honor and keep no faith with him who is sword and shield and victory."

His daughter stepped from the side of her father and faced him. "You have said that our people all perish because they will not keep faith. My father, I think that what you do now may make a difference in whether they keep their promises to him."

Now this little one turned toward the silent elders and was as brave as any warrior on the battlefield. "I believe my father must fulfill his vow to People-Builder exactly as he made it and you must go back and tell all the people what he has done so they will remember. I am not afraid to go to live with People-Builder beyond the sky. All I ask is that you allow me two cycles of the moon to walk the highlands and weep with my friends."

"Your words are so wise and so brave. Certainly you may go."

So the girl and her closest friends climbed the hills and camped beneath a million sparkling stars. The girls laughed and talked and cried. They cried about all that would never be for the daughter of Outcast:

never a husband to hold;

never a child to rock;

never lazy afternoons in which to grow old.

In the early morning the girl walked alone and listened to the wind, and deep in her heart she knew she would experience something better than all she gave up. So she did not flinch when her father bound her in the way he had bound many lambs and laid her on the stone altar and lifted his knife. She passed from the blue planet with a smile of peace.

And every morning thereafter Outcast walked the highlands with People-Builder. He ruled with strength and justice. And through his life many people looked beyond the sky because his daughter had helped him keep his foolish vow.

Still, Outcast could find no rest for himself and not many years later his heart failed under the weight of regrets. Outcast went to find peace by the side of his daughter in the house of People-Builder.

WHEN PASSION
OVERCOMES WISDOM,
JOY IS BRIEF.

CHAPTER 8

THE LONER

The first People of the Sea came as refugees. But they were displaced because their warrior spirit could not settle a place without dominating it. They settled the coastline and rebuilt cities destroyed by Point Man. More trickled in, intelligent traders and master craftsmen with skill to make stronger metal and more dangerous weapons. They took care that their neighbors did not share such knowledge. Five powerful cities grew along the coastal lowlands. They encroached and made ultimatums and bullied the People of the Promise into submission. Their outposts pushed farther inland with their strong arms and stronger swords and fast chariots.

The Sea People took note that the People of the Promise talked much about People-Builder, but they spent more energy making statues of Shining One.

People tired of anarchy welcomed strength.

Most did not care to fight the invaders.

Few found reason to cry to the one beyond the sky.

People-Builder was not totally forgotten. West of the City of Palms a middle-aged couple clung to the words of the one who is always close and always cares. They knew the ancient stories and told them to anyone who would listen. They longed most to tell the stories to a child of their own, but too many summers had passed to hope that their arms would be filled.

The woman still cried out—and one night she was answered. In the darkness stood one who glowed with a fierce and dreadful and wonderful brightness.

"In nine cycles of the moon you will carry a boy child in your arms," said the angel. "He will rule the New Land. He will break the grip of bronze with a grip of iron."

Wonder at this news replaced fear.

"This child will carry blessing and promise and power," continued the angel, "but promises must be kept in return. Three vows are laid upon him. If he fails to keep them, People-Builder will withdraw his blessing."

"I will do all to make certain they are earnestly kept."

"Then, woman, hear what must never be forgotten:

"He must not touch what is dead.

"He must not drink what is fermented.

"He must not cut his hair."

Their boy child grew with vigor. He so enjoyed to be by himself in the hills with People-Builder that he was called Loner. Each day, with his mother, he repeated three vows:

"I will not touch what is dead.

"I will not drink what is fermented.

"I will not cut my hair."

He became a man like none other who had walked the blue planet. His dark features were framed in thick black hair that hung well down his back. His arms and chest and legs were massive and hard, but his heart was gentle and warm and passionate. Loner had no physical weakness, but he had the flaw of one whose life is easy: He did not learn to deny his will and submit to the one who lives beyond the sky. So he saw nothing wrong in his announcement to his parents.

"I have seen the most beautiful of women in all of the blue planet. Father, please arrange my marriage to her."

"From which tribe does this wondrous beauty come?"

"She is a daughter of the sea."

The father's smile faded.

"Then she follows Shining One?"

"She doesn't care about such things. I can teach her. Soon she will walk the ways of People-Builder."

Reluctantly the parents journeyed south. Loner impatiently ran ahead. As he passed carefully tended vineyards, a young lion burst from a thicket. The lion had been lured from the high hills by a flock of sheep. The shepherd had chased him off and he stalked anything.

But this was ill-chosen prey. Loner grabbed his neck and swung him into a tree, breaking his back. He hid the body in the fruit and foliage.

The girl was lovely and her parents prosperous but they had no respect for People-Builder. Loner would not listen. He saw only her deep round eyes. In time a marriage was arranged.

On the way to his wedding Loner noticed the remains of the young lion. Scavengers had picked clean the bones. Now the lion's rib cage was filled with a beehive. Loner pulled the bones apart and scooped a mound of honey, avoiding all but a few stings. He could, after all, do anything.

But in touching the dead lion, he broke the first of his three vows.

Thirty warriors came to Loner's wedding. They had desired this woman and were angry at her choice. They would show their superiority.

Loner enjoyed his thirty new friends. They lifted great cups of brass and offered him the largest. The liquid tasted new and tingling and wonderful.

And so he broke the second of his three vows.

"I will tell you a secret," Loner said, a little loudly. "If you guess my secret, I will give you gifts. And if you can't guess my secret, you must all give me gifts."

"Out of the eater comes something to eat.

"Out of the strong came something sweet."

The thirty warriors had thought that this stupid and drunk strong man would give his secret away in the clue. But this was harder than they had anticipated. What would people say if they were bested by this country ox? After three days, they had no answer. So they cornered Loner's bride. "Persuade him to tell his secret or something may happen to your family."

The girl was terrified. She could tell Loner, and he would probably kill all thirty men but that would make others take revenge. Or she could lie. She chose the second approach.

She broke into tears: "You do not trust me. You do not love me."

This was an unexpected change in mood. He must have done something very wrong.

"What is it?"

"You kept your secret from me."

"I told no one. That is the game."

But the game was no longer fun when his lovely daughter of the sea cried an ocean of tears. He gave in:

"The lion is the eater.

"And honey is sweet.
"But my strength has taken honey from the jaws of the eater."

As the sun sank low the thirty men went to see Loner. Why had she betrayed him? Loner walked west out of the town and out of the valley, leaving the beautiful girl. To avoid disgrace, her father quickly married his daughter to the most handsome of her thirty suitors. Their plan had worked splendidly.

In a few days each of the thirty found a handsome new robe and sandals at his door. But soon thirty wealthy men of the community were discovered. Each had a broken neck. None wore clothes.

The next night fires broke out in fields. Houses burned. Olive trees and grapevines were scorched. Heavy smoke covered the sun and choked the people.

"Who has destroyed our crops?" the king of the Sea People asked the elders.

"One of the People of the Promise," said the elders. "He was angry that his bride was given to another man."

Warriors tracked Loner. But these were his hills. No one found him.

So the warrior captain went to the closest town of the People of the Promise and surrounded it.

"You harbor a bandit," the warrior captain charged.

"We do not," gasped the frightened elders.

"I believe you do," the captain said darkly. "Produce him or nothing will live in this village."

Townspeople slipped by the guards that night.

The next morning a mountain of a man was led toward the Sea People's camp. His hands were bound. Loner looked at the cheering warriors calmly and fearlessly and directly. That night they celebrated while the strong man lay bound in the dark. Finally a drunken execution squad staggered over to deal with their prisoner. But the man they found lying on the ground was a guard—his head split open. Nearby was another, and over there, more.

The soldiers shouted the alarm.

But no one answered.

It could not be. One man could not have killed all. The warriors grabbed their weapons and sprinted into the dark, hearts filled with fear.

At daylight the camp was silent. Only one weary man stirred, eating. At his side lay a heavy piece of donkey's skull, a jawbone broken and bloody and shattered.

"My life belongs to you," said Loner. "You are my strength and my sustenance."

"You are my special one," whispered the wind, "but you have broken two vows. Cling to the third."

For twenty summers Loner led the People of the Promise. The People of the Sea plotted and sent assassins and set ambushes. He escaped each trap. Yet the king knew there was a secret to such strength. He would find it.

In the village market Loner saw her, a maiden so beautiful it broke his heart. She was a weaver in a nearby valley. Loner knew the danger, but danger heightened the adventure. Could any enemy touch him? She hung on his massive arm and asked, "No man has ever had muscles like these. What gives you such strength?"

Loner laughed and picked her up as if she were a doll.

"Tie my hands and bind my feet.

"Use seven bowstrings complete.

"Then I will be yours forever."

A few days later he was asleep when men burst into the house. He awoke to find himself bound in the dark. The woman screamed and he snapped the bindings and sent bodies hurtling. One man lay dead. The rest ran for their lives.

His enemies had learned where he stayed. Well they would not try that again. Loner drifted back to sleep and did not count the seven strings of hide that had bound him. Beauty clouded his thoughts.

Soon her arms stretched around him once more.

"My strong mountain, I wonder if you love me. I have a thought that you are untruthful. I can't imagine bowstrings ever stopping one so powerful as you."

"You have found me out, little one. So I will tell you:

"Bind my feet and wrap my hands,

"Ropes never used, the moment demands.

"Then I will be yours forever."

As the strong man slept, his heartless lover tied his hands and feet with the new ropes. Then she yelled, "Loner, the enemy is upon you!"

He jumped to his feet and effortlessly broke the new ropes. But beauty still clouded his mind.

"I thought I would try your truthfulness. You have lied again. Why won't you tell me this secret?"

Loner looked serious. "I was betrayed once, but you are different.

"Why do you fret and get upset

"when you could be a weaver.

"Take my long hair

"and. . .and weave it there. . . ."

Loner pointed to the large loom.

"and I will be yours forever."

He had almost said the secret but had stopped short. Not many days afterward Loner drank deeply of her oldest wine and dropped off by her loom. She worked the long hair into a tight weave. Warriors once more hid nearby.

"Loner, the enemy is upon you."

The legend awoke with a jerk, stood to his feet and pulled his woven hair from the loom, breaking warp threads and cracking the shuttle.

Yet beauty still clouded his mind. The woman pressed harder. "If you cannot trust me with the secret of your remarkable strength, our love is over."

He almost left her. The game was old and he had no intention of telling her. And he was sick of her anger.

Weeks later he again drank of her best and oldest wine.

"Enough! Why do I have to prove my passion? But I will trust you with my life. One more hint, and we will forget this—

"Cut the tresses from my head.

"Then I will face my greatest dread.

"I shall be yours forever."

Loner lay in a stupor. The soldiers were summoned.

"Bring your sharpest knife to cut his hair. He has told all."

A few hours later Loner heard his lover's voice through a drunken haze. "Loner, the enemy is upon you!"

He staggered up. Yes, it did seem people were all around. Swords, spears. He would make them sorry they had bothered his sleep.

But the warriors did not run away and he could not toss them about. They held and beat him unconscious. Suddenly more pain than he had ever imagined pushed through his eyes.

Then all was black.

Pain, shock, despair. He knew all, but it was too late. He felt his shaved head. His final vow was broken. His strength was gone. He imagined her alone in her house counting thousands of silver coins. And in his damp dungeon, reeling in agony from wounded eyes, the pain of betrayal was greater than the pain of capture.

"Oh People-Builder, how could I have been so foolish?"

Loner's face kept its upward glance and, even without eyes, he looked beyond the sky. A golden light, brighter than the sun, illuminated his darkness. A rainbow more colorful than he had ever seen crossed his vision.

"Your actions have consequences, but I am always close and I will always care," whispered the wind.

Cycles of the moon passed. The People of the Sea had a great holiday. There was much to celebrate, for their great enemy now pushed a grain mill wheel like a donkey. They offered praises to Shining One and drank much wine and begged to see the bald man who once had been strongest on the blue planet.

The leaders gathered in the greatest temple of the land. The wealthy took seats of honor. The king and governors sat with the woman who had brought down the invincible. Thousands crowded around and even got on the roof to watch the spectacle. An ancient serpent crawled from his hole to mock the broken man.

Loner felt the sun on his face and energy surged as they stretched him between two magnificent stone pillars and there secured his arms and legs with heavy bronze shackles. But Loner kept his face skyward. And the betraying woman noticed something and felt uneasy: The hair on Loner's head was matted and dirty, but it was long and black.

Loner whispered, "Bondage-Breaker and Land-Giver and People-Builder. Give me strength to serve you once more."

He rested his back against a pillar and planted his feet firmly against the other. He pushed with more strength than he had ever before felt. And a weak point in one pillar separated into a tiny crack.

One pillar began to move. With so many people on the roof, the shift in the one pillar threw impossible stresses on the other. Now it broke free.

With all his might he shoved outward.

The building trembled and cracks spread across the facade.

The great pillars tipped.

And the last sounds Loner heard were the screams of his captors.

It was said that all those who had kept the Sea People powerful were pulled broken from the rubble. It seemed unbelievable that so many could die in the collapse of a single building. The People of the Promise claimed the body of their leader. Loner was laid beside his parents with great honor.

The People of the Sea still held the New Land. But they would decline until they faded from history, while the legend of Loner spread across the blue planet.

WORDS OFTEN HURT
IF THEY ARE HARSH;
THEY CAN KILL
IF THEY GO UNSAID.

CHAPTER 9

THE KEEPER

Keeper never led soldiers into battle. He never stood alone in combat of arms. Not once did he journey so much as a day's walk from his home. But he was a warrior. He walked with his maker and wrestled for the people in the eternal one's presence. He spent all his life at the Place of Peace protecting the Special Place and the ark of mystery.

It was not the life he had desired. As a child he dreamed of blade ringing against blade as he stood beside Mighty Warrior. He watched men of nearby villages go to fight with Outcast. He spent hours talking with the giant of a man they called Loner. He had not been ashamed to weep when Outcast died of a broken heart and Loner was crushed under the temple by his own folly.

Keeper had always been too heavy and weak for the life of a warrior. So he lived instead in the stories of Garden-Maker and Promise-Keeper and Bondage-Breaker. He loved to learn about his own ancestor, Brother, the first chief keeper of the Special Place. Since General had set apart his brother, the chief keeper had always been a descendant of that family.

It was not an easy calling. He rose before light to walk with People-Builder. He pointed beyond the sky and asked the one who is above all to be patient with the People. He and the keepers under him bound the animals and carried them up to the altar and killed them quickly with a precise cut to the neck. The keepers lifted their arms in praise and confession as the fragrant smoke lifted into the sky. Keeper greeted all who came to sacrifice their spotless newborn lambs. He stood at the entrance and spoke to them kindly and compassionately with the perfect mixture of strength and grace. Among those who followed People-Builder, Keeper was the most loved in all the New Land.

As a leader Keeper reminded people of the words and ways of People-Builder. He drew them to the Place of Peace. He taught truth about the one beyond the sky who holds the stars in his hands. People listened and followed Keeper's words—except two rebels—his own sons:

two sons with dark and deceitful hearts;

two sons who did not respect People-Builder;

two sons who listened to Shining One.

Keeper loved his children. He pointed them to the highlands and beyond the sky. He looked for their turning toward People-Builder. But he knew things were not right. The boys spoke rudely to their mother and defied their father and defiled the Special Place.

When their mother died, their actions grew worse. Keeper gave them work as his assistants. He hoped they would listen as he spoke of the ways of People-Builder. Surely their hearts would soften. They would realize that one was above all; one was truly infinite and eternal and all-powerful. They would see that he was always close and he always cared. They would lower their heads and speak their regrets with sorrow-filled eyes.

But these men looked to another and spoke with him often.

"You hold the opportunity to meet all your desires," hissed an old and familiar voice. "You need only look to me and do my will. Who will stop you? The world is yours."

"Father will stop us."

"Will he? He spends his time with People-Builder and doesn't want to be involved in life."

"But he is good. He is wise."

"He is an old man with his head in old ways. You hold the ways of the future," said the snake as it coiled about their feet. "The people once needed People-Builder but they have outgrown such fables. They must see that following me serves them better."

What the serpent said made sense. So the two began to do whatever they wished. And what they wished became more twisted. They drank too much wine and fought with innocent strangers and seduced women. They stole the sacrifices of people who came to the Special Place. They mocked all that had meaning. Selfishness and violence and anarchy filled their lives.

Shining One gloated at how faithfully they followed his every whim.

The people grew angry and disgusted as they watched the rebellious sons become more violent and vicious. Farmers talked in their fields and shepherds in the hills and women in the market. Keeper heard. His heart sank and his hopes shattered.

Keeper wept.

But he said little.

And he did nothing.

"Why do you follow the ways of anarchy?" he asked the two men who stood silently before him.

"People say you steal from them, but worse—you steal from People-Builder."

The two men looked at their weak, fat father. He no longer seemed good or wise or important. He was unsophisticated and backward. "We will do what we want," they agreed, as they turned their backs on the old man and walked from the Special Place.

Keeper wept.

But he said little.

And he did nothing.

Every day Keeper sacrificed two spotless newborn lambs for his sons, and tears wet the lambs upon the altar. "Why won't they follow you? Will they never stop resisting?" He knew he must take his sons' authority away. But in the end he did not.

One day a hand rested on his bent and weary shoulders. It was Keeper's assistant, looking sad and hesitant.

"I heard a voice in the night," he began. "The voice gave a message for you—a message from People-Builder."

Keeper lifted his eyes. Was People-Builder now speaking through others to him?

"Tell me all. I want to hear."

"People-Builder will cut short the days of your sons because they show no respect for what is right and good and pure. He said: 'Those who honor me I will honor. Those who mock me I will mock. And the keeper of my Special Place has feared to defend my honor. He has joined his sons in shame. He is faithful in easy matters but will not make the hard decisions. I will now look elsewhere for one to stand against all my enemies.' "

Keeper hung his head low. He loved his sons, but he could not save them from themselves. Instead he shared in their guilt.

As Keeper grew older and remembered nearly a hundred summers, he could no longer live as he had in his younger life.

His middle became rounder.

His walk was more halting.

His eyes no longer held light.

The People of the Sea saw his weakness. They had become stronger, and they now openly attacked the New Land. A day's journey west of the Place of Peace the warriors of People-Builder held their ground, but soon many lay without breath.

The New Land had not seen such a loss in many summers. The People of the Promise looked to the highlands and cried out, "One above all, why didn't you go before us in battle?"

"You didn't come to me," said the wind.

"We have come to you now," begged the people.

"Have you?"

"Yes, but we must know for certain that you will stand at our side in battle."

"There is one way. Walk with me. Follow my ways, and I will be your sword and shield and strength," whistled the wind.

There had to be a more certain way than that. What had Point Man done to conquer the land? Yes, the People of the Promise had carried People-Builder's presence—in the ark of mystery—before them.

"If the ark leads the way, we will win the battle," they decided.

They hurried to tell Keeper.

"No, you could not have heard such a command from People-Builder. You desire reassurance because you are afraid," cried Keeper. "Don't listen to Shining One. The ark must stay in the Most Hallowed Chamber."

"We must be led into battle once again by People-Builder, and People-Builder is in the ark of mystery!" A company of warriors started for the Place of Peace led by Keeper's two sons.

"How preposterous to put People-Builder in a box. You have lost the point of the ark."

But the people did as they wished.

"You can't do this!" shouted Keeper with all the voice he could muster. "The ark will not give you the presence of People-Builder!"

"Quiet down, old man," interrupted one of his own sons with contempt. "The warriors need the ark and we will deliver it to the battlefield."

The sons carried the ark from its sacred place and led the warriors back to the battlefield. When the procession entered the camp, the people stared in amazement as the sun made the angels glow. Heat radiated from the beautiful creatures and as the rays struck the golden wings they seemed to flutter.

As it passed, the People of the Promise shouted with joy and hope and awe.

"Why do they cheer?" asked the warriors of the sea. "We are about to crush them!"

"They have seen the ark of mystery," said a spy. "The ark has been moved into their camp so People-Builder can lead them to victory."

"No one can stand against People-Builder," said the enemy warriors. "We will die."

"We are warriors of Shining One. Live or die we will not run before his rival."

The People of the Promise fought with new confidence. And the warriors of the sea fought with a strength born of fear. The armies collided with noise and furor. All the valiant men around the ark fell. As darkness fell, the surviving soldiers fled to the hills.

The battle was lost.

The two sons were dead.

The ark of mystery was in enemy hands.

A young messenger raced to the Place of Peace where Keeper sat waiting. He heard the weary footfalls of the messenger approach.

"What news of the ark?"

"The battle was very great, father Keeper. Losses were heavy."

"The ark of mystery?" repeated Keeper.

"I saw your sons carrying the ark bravely into the midst of the fighting. They fell side by side in the heat of the battle and I did not see them rise."

"Please, my child, what of the ark?"

"The People of the Sea have taken its glory from our midst."

Pain filled Keeper's sightless eyes. "Shining One holds the precious ark of mystery. All things are lost. I have betrayed the people and People-Builder and even my wayward sons."

His face paled. His body shook. He fell backwards and his breath was gone.

Many things were lost. The people mourned their warriors and Keeper. They mourned the ark, for they sensed that a greatness had left them. The future looked dismal. Without the ark could there be a Special Place? Without the Special Place could there be the Place of Peace? Without the Place of Peace would People-Builder dwell among them?"

Some knew. . .knew that People-Builder was not gone because the ark was absent. . .knew that the one beyond the sky had not left them.

What no one knew was that a new era was coming. The world would change to an age of kings and kingdoms, and soon a new home for the ark of mystery.

The two rebel sons had not held the way of the future.

Nor did Shining One.

TREATING
IMPORTANT THINGS LIGHTLY
RISKS MORE THAN
THE THINGS THEMSELVES.

CHAPTER 10

THE SPEAKER

For twenty-five summers Speaker had worked at Keeper's side. Now the old man was dead and his sons were dead and the ark was gone. Speaker's mind reeled. The Special Place was his home. Keeper was his family. Speaker's parents had asked People-Builder for a child. His mother had promised: "Fill my womb with a son and I will give that boy-child back to you. He will keep the three vows of Loner:

"He will not touch what is dead.

"He will not drink what is fermented.

"He will not cut his hair."

A son was born, and when he was still quite young, his parents brought him to the Special Place. Keeper took the child in his wrinkled hands and kissed his forehead. "His words will be strong and true. People-Builder will speak through him. He shall be known as Speaker!"

But it was People-Builder who had spoken on a blustery night.

"Speaker."

The child often served Keeper at night. He rubbed his eyes and went to the next chamber. "Father Keeper. What may I do for you?"

The old man had roused from sleep to mumble, "I didn't call you. Go and lie down."

So Speaker returned to sleep.

"Speaker."

The boy awoke once more. It had been louder that time. Could he have imagined it? He returned to the side of Keeper. "Father Keeper. I am certain you called. What may I do for you?"

Keeper turned dim eyes toward the boy thoughtfully. "I did not call. Go and lie down."

Speaker returned to his bed.

"Speaker!"

He was still awake, and the call was unmistakable.

"Father Keeper. The wind seems to speak my name."

"When the wind speaks your name, answer. On the wind speaks he who holds stars in his hands. Tell him: 'I am yours and I am listening.' "

This time Speaker lay still and closed his eyes and waited.

"Speaker."

"I am yours and I am listening."

"I will come to you many times. Will you follow my words and be true to your three vows?"

A submissive life answered that question. Speaker walked each morning with People-Builder. He answered the call of his name in the darkness. His actions responded: "I am yours and I am listening."

Now he needed to listen intently. Judgment had fallen on Keeper and his sons. The people were without a leader. He stood before the Special Place. The large flat-roofed tent was beautiful with its rich linen cloth of blue and purple and scarlet, embroidered with angels. Speaker turned and looked across the valley.

The view was magnificent.

The landscape was breathtaking.

The danger was great, for the enemy would soon come.

He felt panic as he realized that the thousands of sea soldiers would certainly set out for the Place of Peace. Speaker called to those who served Keeper. The fastest and strongest ran to find the warriors who hid in the hills. The Place of Peace must be protected. Men were gathered for a hasty defense. They fought stubbornly but could not stop the Sea People. Like a wave the enemy swept across the plain. The People of the Promise fled.

Savage warriors burst into the courtyard of the Special Place expecting a magnificent temple and great riches. But nothing was there. The tent and wooden frame, the copper altar and basin, the golden table and candlesticks and incense stand—all were gone. Sturdy wagons stealthily moved a precious cargo south. Those who looked back saw flames from their homes light the sky. Enemy warriors had slashed and broken and smashed whatever they found. The Place of Peace existed no longer. Pain tore at Speaker's heart. The people stopped long enough to share his sorrow.

The Place of Peace was rubble.

The Special Place was homeless.

The ark of mystery was gone.

In one of the five powerful cities of the Sea People, the victors laid their prize of conquest before a stone statue of the ancient serpent in the temple of Shining One.

At first light, the servants of Shining One found their stone statue toppled. It lay on its face before the ark. Its head was broken off. The priests quickly removed the ark from the temple.

The golden ark sat in the street, surrounded by people who looked at the angels with a mixture of curiosity and fear. As the sun touched the roof of the sky, the ark began to glow and the people stepped back. The wings seemed to move and everyone ran for their homes.

At the angelic signal, mice invaded the city from the surrounding fields. They ate the grain and spoiled the food. Their fleas carried the most terrible of diseases. Within days, tumor-like swellings appeared on the people's bodies. They suffered fever and discolored skin and coughing. Then death. As carts collected the dead, the elders ordered the ark from the city.

"These angels bring destruction," said the head elder.

"It is a coincidence," said the king. "The ark has shown itself to be without power."

"Take it away!"

The ark went to another city. Once again the angel wings beckoned mice, and people began to die horribly. So the soldiers moved the ark to a third city and to a fourth city and finally to the fifth city.

"Take this curse from us!" pleaded the elders of the fifth city.

"Send it back," said the priests of Shining One. "Our possession of the golden angels offends People-Builder. We must return it with tokens of apology. If each city gives a golden mouse and a golden tumor it will show our sincerity."

"It is a coincidence," complained the king. "The ark has no power. We should melt it down to make statues for Shining One."

"Shining One loves his statues," agreed the priest. "But if People-Builder is infinite and eternal and all-powerful, he could wash us all into the Great Sea."

"I must know," declared the king.

A test was devised. A cart was built on which the ark rested. The golden mice and tumors were placed beside it. Two unbroken cows were brought from a nearby herd to the east. They kicked and pulled against one another in anger as the yoke was placed around their necks. Finally they were hitched to the cart.

Would they turn it over and kick out of their harness?

Would they turn toward their stalls where their calves were hungry?

Or would they take the ark back to its country?

The cows became docile and turned neither to the right nor to the left. They walked directly west into the New Land.

The king now knew the truth. His people had been deceived and the serpent had offered no protection from the power of People-Builder.

But in the end, the king did not turn from Shining One.

The two cows pulled the cart into a valley ripe with wheat. The workers approached the cart that had no driver. They looked closer and word spread and people gathered.

The crowd pressed close. Five or six men carefully lifted the ark of mystery from the cart. Women laid out woolen blankets so the ark wouldn't touch the dusty road. The crowd pressed closer.

"Open it!" shouted one of the men at the back of the throng.

The lid was heavy and they could only slide it back a little, but it was enough for a peek within the shadows.

Two stone tablets with the ten words.

A golden jar of morning bread.

A shepherd's staff that had blossomed.

But now the ark began to glow and a mist filled the box. Lightning flashed outward from the golden angels, killing those who had looked within. The lid slammed shut and the noise stopped and the glowing cooled. Seventy died. The rest ran from the ark's fury.

When Speaker heard of the return of the ark and the deaths of the people he moved the ark to a small hillside town west of the City of Palms. There it stayed, unopened and undefiled, until the time of the Shepherd King.

The Special Place was now at the City of Priests. It could be seen from the City of Palms. The silver braces were set and the wooden frame lifted and the beautiful linen walls placed. The courtyard was measured and the copper altar positioned. The sanctuary was complete.

But none came. None even cared. The sea warriors ruled. The People of the Promise listened to Shining One.

"People-Builder has lost his power," hissed the snake. "Look around you. The Place of Peace is no more. Make me statues and turn your back on People-Builder."

Speaker traveled the land and spoke the words of the one above all, but few listened. His heart grew heavy, but he was renewed each morning as he walked with him who holds stars in his hands.

After twenty summers the people grew tired of Shining One's empty promises and arrogant anarchy. So they turned to Speaker and truly listened. "Shining One will never set you free. Return to People-Builder and the one beyond the sky will break your bondage again."

The people smashed their statues. Then they gathered in a great assembly south of the ruins of the Place of Peace. "Speak for us," implored the people. "Tell the one above the sky that we wish to be his people and to follow where he leads."

The warriors of the sea came to stop the gathering. When the People of the Sea were seen in the distance, the people cried out in terror: "What shall we do?"

"Stand by the side of People-Builder and he will stand at your side." Speaker sacrificed a spotless newborn lamb. He lifted his hands with the sweet smoke. "Be our victory," he said.

"Victory is yours," came the reply on the wind.

They set their lines on the high ridge and waited.

"We can't fight so many," said one of the men.

The enemy moved closer and the young men grew restless.

"We don't have a chance against so many."

"Hold your ground!" cried Speaker. "People-Builder is our sword and shield and strength. Impossibilities never stopped People-Builder from keeping his word!" shouted Speaker up and down the lines. The power of his voice quieted his men.

With a cry, the sea soldiers surged up the steep ridge.

"Steady!" said Speaker. "Don't move!"

The ground began to rumble under the feet of the charging soldiers. It trembled and shook and heaved until each man was thrown from his feet. Swords and shields were discarded as they clung to the ground.

Then all was silent.

"Attack!" yelled Speaker.

The enemy stumbled away, leaving their weapons. The warriors of the promise rushed forward with confidence in one who shaped thunder and shifted the ground. The People of the Promise cheered and the warriors shouted, "He is our victory!"

Summers passed and the people listened to the words of Speaker. Then the elders met with him.

"The Sea People have a king and the Plains People have a king and the Desert People have a king. Why don't we have a king?"

"People-Builder is our king," said Speaker.

"We want a king we can touch and see, like the kings around us!"

"Kings can be costly and cruel. They are interested in women and wealth and power. They kill and force you to labor at their whim. Once there is a king, everything changes."

"Find a king for us, or we will seek one ourselves."

People-Builder heard the people sadly. What they wanted was not what they needed. But he would guide his people through good and bad kings.

The days of leaders would pass and the days of kings begin. Five hundred summers had passed since a young girl had hidden a baby in the tall reeds of the Wide River. Since then great leaders had pointed beyond the sky. One had looked to Bondage-Breaker and another to Land-Giver and eight had cried to People-Builder.

But the people were restless. They wished to stretch toward a new destiny. Before them lay great glory and peril and tragedy. People-Builder had built the People of the Promise. He would remain with them.

For he was always close and he would always care.

EPILOGUE

The fire had collapsed to coals and ashes while the old man spoke. The old man stood silent in shadow, but his final words echoed. They too had experienced him who was always close and would always care. At no time was that clearer than when the wrinkled man told his stories.

A crystal moon had completed its cycle and returned to its full circle of light. For thirty nights the small attentive crowd sat on the ground to meditate on General and Point Man and Mighty Warrior—absorbing eternal truths their lives held.

The girl child approached and tugged on his robe. The old man bent down.

"Why did they want a king?" she asked.

"People find it easier to follow what they can see," said the old man.

"I know the wind is real and I can't see it," said the girl child.

"The mightiest forces can't be seen," said the storyteller.

The young one looked up wisely and nodded. Her grandfather wrapped a simple wool blanket around her shoulders and kissed her forehead.

"I'll see you tomorrow," said the old man.

"Can I come with you to wake the sun with the one above all? Can I be with you to welcome the night with stories?" asked the girl child.

"Both," said the grandfather with a devoted smile. "Tomorrow we'll do both."

More stories would come of courage and love and battles and betrayal. Only one thing would be the same—he who holds stars in his hands would be as close as the wind. But he would go by other names.

A light breeze touched the faces of the young and the old while the one beyond the sky touched their hearts with peace.

BEHIND THE STORIES . . .

Bible texts from Exodus through 1 Samuel inspired these stories. The corresponding Bible passages are:

The Baby	Exodus 1:1–2:9
The Killing	Exodus 2:10–25
The Call	Exodus 3–4
The Disasters	Exodus 5–10
The Night of Nights	Exodus 11:1–12:20
The Crossing	Exodus 12:31–15:21
The Complaints	Exodus 15:22–17:16
The Mountain	Exodus 19–20:32
The Special Place	Exodus 33–40; Leviticus 8–10
The Edge	Exodus 18; Numbers 10–12
The Scouts	Numbers 13–14
The Wandering	Numbers 16–17
The Final Year	Numbers 20
The Sorcerer	Numbers 22–25, 31
The Passing Away	Deuteronomy
The Innkeeper	Joshua 1–2
The Victory	Joshua 3–6
The Silver and Gold	Joshua 7–8
The Lie	Joshua 9–10
The Place of Peace	Joshua 11–24
The Lion	Judges 1–3:10
The Outsider	Judges 3:11–13; Ruth
The Left Hand	Judges 3:14–30
The Beekeeper's Wife	Judges 4–5
The Mighty Warrior	Judges 6–8
The Renegade	Judges 9
The Outcast	Judges 10–12
The Loner	Judges 13–16
The Keeper	1 Samuel 2:12–36; 4
The Speaker	1 Samuel 1–2:11; 3; 5–8